Praise for
The 27 Challenges Managers Face

"Whether you have been managing people for twenty-seven days or twenty-seven years, Bruce Tulgan's research and book will prove a practical and invaluable guide for meeting specific challenges and managing for success."
—**Ray Kotcher,** chairman and senior partner, Ketchum

"Management is basic work, but hard work. We applied Bruce Tulgan's principles of Management 101 to rapidly turn our organization into a focused execution machine. In *The 27 Challenges Managers Face*, Bruce provides a pocket guide and a comprehensive overview of how to manage, every day, for business impact. Whether you are an experienced manager or taking on your first direct reports, whether you are trying to be a better manager or improve an entire organization's ability to manage and execute, Bruce's guide is the manual you need."
—**Geoffrey Crouse,** CEO and president, Cord Blood Registry

"*The 27 Challenges Managers Face* is a good read for managers and people who lead people. Tackle the recurring daily challenges of leading yourself and others by rediscovering fundamental principles of communication and management."
—**Sylvia B. Vogt,** president, Carnegie Bosch Institute,
Tepper School of Business, Carnegie Mellon University

"Bruce Tulgan will refocus you. His scholarly research and anecdotal style will make an immediate impact on developing talent. *The 27 Challenges Managers Face* is a must-read for any company that believes it is their people who make the difference."
—**Keith A. Hoogland,** president, Family Video

"*The 27 Challenges Managers Face* is a must-read for every manager on your team. These fundamentals are the basis for running an outstanding organization, and Bruce Tulgan gives you the steps you need to develop a high-performing organization. Every manager should read this book, whether you've been leading an organization for days or decades!"
—**Deb Dulsky,** chief commercial officer, HomeServe USA

"I've been a fan of Bruce Tulgan and his work for over fifteen years. *The 27 Challenges Managers Face* is a very well-written and insightful guide. Whether you're a new or seasoned manager, Bruce's book offers step-by-step guidance and practical advice. Bruce really nails it, and my only wish is that this book had been written years ago, when I first became a manager."
—**Lorie Valle-Yañez,** vice president, chief diversity
officer, MassMutual Financial Group

"Like Studs Terkel before him, Bruce Tulgan was educated as a lawyer but discovered his real passion in the study of how people work and manage. Bruce brings that passion to life with *The 27 Challenges Managers Face* and reminds us that Management 101 is easy to understand in theory, but easy to forget on Monday mornings."
—**Hank Harris,** president and CEO, FMI Corporation

"*The 27 Challenges Managers Face* is a practical, smart, easy-to-use guide from one of the clearest thinkers in the field. Bruce Tulgan has done it again, creating a must-read compendium for handling the most common to the most vexing management challenges. It's all here."
—**Alan Greene,** executive vice president, business
head, US Investment Services and Institutional
Investor Services, State Street Corporation

"Bruce Tulgan was the original voice of reason about how to manage the next generation of leadership. In *The 27 Challenges Managers Face*, he provides an immensely insightful yet practical guide for managers of any generation. Bruce has always based his work on years of careful research, thousands of interviews and focus studies, and deep experience coaching managers from the front lines of fast food to the officers of the elite US military. He writes as he speaks, pulls no punches, is immensely entertaining, and always leaves his audience better prepared to succeed as managers."
—**Joni Thomas Doolin,** founder and CEO, People Report

"*The 27 Challenges Managers Face* gives direct and straightforward ways to handle challenges. Bruce Tulgan's continued focus on the basic fundamentals, the importance of one-on-ones, and easy-to-understand examples is not only refreshing but will yield results."
 —**Robert Werk,** senior vice president, operations, CraftWorks Restaurants & Breweries

"Bruce Tulgan has hit another home run! *The 27 Challenges Managers Face* is simple and easy to read yet relevant and practical in application. This book is designed to be referenced again and again, to address the classic challenges of getting results through others. No matter how seasoned a manager is, these principles will help fulfill the responsibilities of leadership in the most effective way possible. A must-read and a must-practice for today's new and experienced managers."
 —**Sharon McPherson,** director of training, On The Border Mexican Grill & Cantina

"In his always clear and insightful style, Bruce Tulgan puts forth practical and easy-to-follow solutions for the most common supervisory challenges facing all managers, regardless of industry. *The 27 Challenges Managers Face* is helpful for new supervisors and veterans of management alike. Bruce researched in the workplace to hear from real managers where their greatest challenges lay, and he shares the basic solutions in an appetizing and easy-to-digest way, making this a good reference book to keep on the shelf after reading."
 —**Doug Gammon,** vice president, human resources and training, Black Angus Steakhouses

"I honestly believe anyone interested in being a better manager could benefit from *The 27 Challenges Managers Face*. If they had a particular need for advice, they could pick the book up, look at the table of contents, and find help with a solution. I loved this book."
 —**Judy Irwin,** vice president, human resources and training, Golden Corral

"Based on decades of firsthand interview research, Bruce Tulgan's coaching enabled our general managers and store managers to communicate more easily and effectively with, motivate, and develop their line staff, notably improving overall shop performance. *The 27 Challenges Managers Face* will help owners and managers connect authentically with staff, overcoming the chronic misperception by staff that they are not seen or understood, enabling a positive working atmosphere critical to growing your business."
 —**Doug Bell,** president, Grasslands Uruguay, and
  retired president, Supercuts Owners Association

"What sets Bruce Tulgan's work apart from other management books is that he provides real-world advice for real-world management challenges. *The 27 Challenges Managers Face*, like his others, is meant to be consulted again and again. Don't stick this one on your reference shelf; keep it close at hand, and watch your management performance improve."
 —**John Bissell,** executive vice president, Greylock Federal Credit Union

"*The 27 Challenges Managers Face* brings great insight for executives at any level and phase in their career. This is practical information you can use now to inform your strategies moving forward for the way you manage people and how you are managed, as well. A comprehensive primer on managing people with heart and integrity, while still getting bottom-line results for your company, *The 27 Challenges Managers Face* is a book you should have within reach at your desk."
 —**Daniel Butler,** vice president, community integration, National Retail Federation

"First Bruce Tulgan gave us permission to manage; now he tells us when and how to execute the fundamentals, based upon years of experience and success. *The 27 Challenges Managers Face* is for the seasoned executive as well as the new manager and will make a lasting difference in your life and the lives of others."
 —**L. Gary Boomer,** CEO, Boomer Consulting, Inc.

"Bruce Tulgan forces managers to ask ourselves what our job truly is, and then enumerates simple—though in no way simplistic—steps for us to take to do that job. Management is work, and *The 27 Challenges Managers Face* removes the excuse so many of us use as a crutch when those who perform under us underperform—that the fault lies not in ourselves, but in our stars."
 —**Homer Robinson,** president and CEO, Kaiserman Company

"Once again, Bruce Tulgan has provided us with a back-to-basics fundamentals book, packed with research and practical solutions. *The 27 Challenges Managers Face* will be a go-to reference and solution guide for years to come. Bruce's writing style invites the reader to embrace management challenges and be much better for it."

　　—**Carl George,** CEO, Carl George Advisory, LLC, and former CEO, Clifton Gunderson LLP

"Bruce Tulgan continues to be my guru of management! *The 27 Challenges Managers Face* provides examples and research and makes it easy to find the right material when facing a management issue. I'll use it to coach other managers and help them improve their confidence and performance."

　　—**Janet Kyle Altman,** marketing principal, Kaufman Rossin

"*The 27 Challenges Managers Face* is yet another example of Bruce Tulgan's ability to identify the issues managers face and offer specific action steps to help them lead their organizations to success. Leaders, managers, and employees at all levels will benefit by reading this book, and based on their current situation, can decide which chapter to tackle first. The book is a great read and a resource all managers should turn to as situations arise."

　　—**Howard C. Fero,** professor of leadership, Albertus Magnus College,
　　and coauthor, *Lead Me Out to the Ballgame*

"Bruce Tulgan creates practical advice and solutions leaders can use to engage employees and deliver results. He understands the challenges modern managers face, and by helping them communicate more effectively, he prepares leaders to handle tough issues and help people achieve their highest level of performance."

　　—**Jennifer Russo,** director, corporate communications, Copper Group, Rio Tinto

"Many of our managers at Westar Energy have found a mentor in Bruce Tulgan. As we work as a company on raising the level of conversation between managers and employees, we found that Bruce's message of talk about the work was particularly useful. After two visits and a series of weekly online messages, it's quite commonplace at Westar for our leaders to reference Bruce Tulgan."

　　—**Diane Owen,** lead training representative, Westar Energy

"*The 27 Challenges Managers Face* exposes the root management problem, refreshingly admits that there is no easy fix, and then provides nuanced advice that can be individually tailored by each manager. Like others in the field, Bruce Tulgan offers numerous tips, but where Tulgan provides significant added value is in his distinguishing between the application of solid management practices that generate real and lasting results and merely going through the motions."

　　—**Steve Katz,** principal, Fish & Richardson

"Bravo! I use Bruce's back-to-basics principles in managing my direct reports and am a big supporter of his work. *The 27 Challenges Managers Face* will be a great reference for managers as they come across various situations."

　　—**George Wilson,** president, Barriere Construction

"*The 27 Challenges Managers Face* is essential reading for managers. Too many managers are operating on autopilot, waiting for a crisis to happen before reacting. Bruce Tulgan rightly emphasizes critical fundamentals, especially around effective communication, that stop the vicious cycle of managing by crisis. MBA students often ask us what the key elements of good management are—they're contained in this cogent, well-argued book."

　　—**Donald E. Gibson,** dean and professor of management, Charles F.
　　Dolan School of Business, Fairfield University

"Bruce Tulgan demonstrates how managers can break the cycle of firefighting and learn to perform meaningful management that benefits the manager, the employees, and the organization. A good manager will go back to *The 27 Challenges Managers Face* time and time again to keep the management structure operating smoothly and effectively."

　　—**Colonel Craig Price,** superintendent, South Dakota Highway Patrol

"Bruce Tulgan hit a home run with this one! He speaks the truth and provides clear, concise management advice. *The 27 Challenges Managers Face* will become my desktop guidebook for helping leaders at all levels manage their way to more effective organizations and better results."
    —**Lisa Beutel,** executive director, Center for Leadership, University of Dayton

"*The 27 Challenges Managers Face* continues to deliver the effective and useful insight I expect from Bruce Tulgan. It is a must for your management toolbox!"
    —**Jon Morrison,** vice president, vehicle dynamics and controls,
    global, WABCO Vehicle Control Systems

"*The 27 Challenges Managers Face* offers great insights into undermanagement. Many of my clients complain about bosses being too hands off, which results in employees who hate their jobs and want to leave because they don't have ongoing, quality communication and feedback from their managers. Each of the twenty-seven scenarios are rich with nuggets on how to navigate the most common people management issues."
    —**Katie Weiser,** former global director, training and development,
    Deloitte Consulting, and CEO, Katie Weiser Coaching

"Once again, Bruce Tulgan takes the essential but often overwhelming responsibility of getting work done through others and breaks it into understandable, commonsense steps. *The 27 Challenges Managers Face* is another great tool."
    —**D. J. Zarnick,** vice president, human resources, The Henry M. Jackson
    Foundation for the Advancement of Military Medicine, Inc.

"*The 27 Challenges Managers Face* covers a broad range of the most essential management topics. Based on research with hundreds of thousands of managers and presented in the inspirational way only Bruce Tulgan can do, this book is the equivalent of having your own mentor. Every manager will become a better manager for it."
    —**Jill Kilroy,** assistant vice president, learning and development,
    Horace Mann Companies

"*The 27 Challenges Managers Face* is a practical, research-based approach to managing one of an organization's most important resources—people. Bruce Tulgan once again combines research and best practices to create a book of solutions. New and experienced managers alike will benefit."
    —**Tani Bialek,** director, national learning and professional development, McGladrey LLP

"*The 27 Challenges Managers Face* covers it all, with valuable insight for managers everywhere. It reminds us that to manage well is to manage often. Managing is a commitment, but one that delivers dividends daily, and Bruce Tulgan enthusiastically encourages us to recommit ourselves to our colleagues and ourselves. The tools are simple, the work hard, and the rewards great."
    —**Jeffrey R. Katz,** partner, Ropes & Gray LLP

"Like any other skill, managing people requires a mastery of the fundamentals. In *The 27 Challenges Managers Face,* Bruce Tulgan presents situations we all face and reminds us how to apply those fundamentals. This book is a mandatory addition to every manager's toolbox."
    —**Arturo M. Hernandez,** vice president, engineering, Grote Industries

"At Chick-fil-A, we've always felt that those who lead must first serve. Bruce Tulgan's book is a great reminder of how to serve well through managing well. So many of today's challenges in organizations can find their beginning and end in the same place: people management. *The 27 Challenges Managers Face* is a great review of the fundamentals of great people management, and how to make them a part of your everyday life."
    —**Andy Lorenzen,** senior director, organizational development, Chick-fil-A, Inc.

THE 27 CHALLENGES MANAGERS FACE

Step-by-Step Solutions to (Nearly)
All of Your Management Problems

Bruce Tulgan

JB JOSSEY-BASS™
A Wiley Brand

Published by Jossey-Bass
A Wiley Brand
One Montgomery Street, Suite 1200, San Francisco, CA 94104-4594
www.josseybass.com

Jossey-Bass books and products are available through most bookstores. To contact Jossey-Bass directly call our Customer Care Department within the U.S. at 800-956-7739, outside the U.S. at 317-572-3986, or fax 317-572-4002.

Wiley publishes in a variety of print and electronic formats and by print-on-demand. Some material included with standard print versions of this book may not be included in e-books or in print-on-demand. If this book refers to media such as a CD or DVD that is not included in the version you purchased, you may download this material at http://booksupport.wiley.com. For more information about Wiley products, visit www.wiley.com.

Library of Congress Cataloging-in-Publication Data

Tulgan, Bruce.
  The 27 challenges managers face : step-by-step solutions to (nearly) all of your management problems / Bruce Tulgan.
    pages cm
  Includes index.
  ISBN 978-1-118-72559-7 (hardback); ISBN 978-1-118-93501-9 (pdf);
  ISBN 978-1-118-93500-2 (epub)
    1. Management. 2. Communication in management. I. Title. II. Title: Twenty-seven challenges managers face.
  HD30.3.T85 2014
  658—dc23

                                                                2014016518

Printed in the United States of America
FIRST EDITION
HB Printing   SKY10024581_012921

This book is dedicated to
Chris Glowacki and Krissy Campbell
and their entire extended family, especially their children,
Lily, Albert, Herbie, and Stella

CONTENTS

THE 27 CHALLENGES MANAGERS FACE

A Note on How to Use This Book

When I talk about the 27 challenges, people often ask me, "Why are there 27 challenges, instead of 26 or 28 or some other number?"

This book is based on twenty years of workplace research conducted by my company, RainmakerThinking, Inc. We've asked hundreds of thousands of managers, in our management seminars, focus groups, interviews, and surveys, some version of this open-ended question: "Which employee situations are most challenging for you as a manager?" Despite the diversity of people and situations, the same basic challenges come up repeatedly. In fact, more than 90 percent of responses over the years refer to these same 27 challenges.

This book is intentionally designed to be used and reused as a reference book—a hands-on management tool you may go back to over and over again throughout your career as a leader, manager, or supervisor. As you'll see in the table of contents, the 27 challenges are not enumerated in order of frequency or difficulty, but rather, grouped in seven chapters based on the larger themes they have in common. I encourage you to go ahead and skip right to the specific challenge you are facing today.

Once you've solved that problem, you may feel tempted to leave this book on your shelf until the next challenge. However, you should consider reading the whole book from beginning to end. Here's why: It turns out that when things are going wrong in a management relationship, almost always the common denominator is unstructured, low-substance, hit-or-miss communication. And almost always the solution comes from applying the fundamentals of management. Throughout the book, you'll see—one challenge at a time—how the most effective managers apply the fundamentals of management to gain control of any situation with a step-by-step solution to the problem at hand. So reading the whole thing from beginning to end is like putting yourself through management fundamentals boot camp. Then go ahead and put it on your shelf until you need a refresher on your next real-life challenge.

However you choose to use this book, please use it well and use it strong!

CHAPTER ONE

The Fundamentals Are All You Need

You walk into your weekly team meeting expecting the standard updates around the table. Some people are more prepared than others. Not enough information from some, too much from others. Digressions. Side conversations. Devices. One hour turns into two.

You sometimes think: "Why do we even have these team meetings?" After all, everyone touches base with everybody on the team almost daily. There is an open door policy. If something comes up, you let each other know as needed. You talk and email with each other all day long.

Nonetheless, the meeting begins as usual. Until it quickly surfaces that very important Project Q is off track and behind schedule. How could this be? You've been checking in with everybody regularly, one-on-one, on top of the weekly team meeting.

It's not clear what happened. Maybe there was a change in specifications that wasn't fully communicated. Perhaps a resource constraint got in the way, a technology glitch, or human error? Somebody must have dropped the ball—internally or externally. Is there anyone who can be held accountable? Mr. Red has dropped the ball before.

There are a lot of moving parts with Project Q. Now changes must be made throughout, changes that will require rework by counterparts in another group in another department. They will not be happy.

Time, resources, energy, and money have been wasted. There is blaming, complaining, explaining. Everything has been harder since the team recently lost its most valuable player, Ms. Platinum. And her replacement, Ms. Bronze, is still not fully up to speed.

You spring into action, and the firefighting ensues. You have a series of one-on-one huddles with the team members you know you can count on in a jam. You take over some responsibilities yourself—including begging the counterparts in the other groups in the other departments to redo their parts. There are some quick stand-up meetings and long hours of heavy lifting. The crisis is handled, and Project Q is back on track.

When you figure out exactly what happened, there will probably be some very difficult conversations, and there will be consequences. Some people might lose their jobs. Even if Mr. Red is not to blame, it's about time you really spoke to Mr. Red about his stubbornly inconsistent performance.

Once you finally get everything back on track, you are way behind on your other responsibilities. So are your employees. But things are mostly back to normal.

You touch base with everybody almost daily. They know your door is always open. If something comes up, you let each other know as needed. You talk and email with each other all day long. In any event, you will catch up with everyone in the next team meeting.

■ ■ ■

Any manager will tell you: firefighting is part of the job. It's very hard to break the cycle, because when there is an urgent problem, it simply must be addressed. Things do go wrong—fires occur. If you are the manager, you are in charge. You lead the fight. Everybody has to grab a bucket and help fight the fire. But it's usually difficult, time-consuming work. By the time you are done, you are way behind on all of the other work you were supposed to be doing.

Many managers have asked themselves this question: How do I make any real progress when there are so many fires to put out?

The question you should be asking is this: How many of the most frequently occurring "fires" can be prevented altogether or largely avoided, or have their impact substantially mitigated? In advance? Way in advance? And every step of the way?

The answer is most of them.

How? By consistently practicing the fundamentals, very well. That means maintaining an ongoing schedule of high-quality one-on-one dialogues with every single person you manage. High-quality means highly structured and highly substantive: ongoing, regular, scheduled, frequent, with a clear execution focus, specific to the individual, and two-way conversation. These are not the so-called "crucial conversations" when things go wrong, but regular check-ins when everything is going great, or not so great, or even just average. This insight is based on twenty years of in-depth research on supervisory relationships in the workplace. What's amazing is that so few managers in the real world consistently practice the fundamentals very well. What's even more amazing is that so many managers think they are already doing it, when they are not.

Look at the manager of Project Q, just described. At first glance, he appears to be attending reasonably well to the fundamentals of management 101: Holding regular team meetings, touching base with his employees almost daily, open door policy, and ongoing visibility by email and telephone.

That's what makes this problem so complicated: the manager is following the right steps—going through the right motions. What else could he be doing? And if you had asked him just before Project Q fell apart, he probably would have said, "Everything is going just fine."

The manager in this story is like the vast majority of managers at all levels in organizations of all shapes and sizes. This manager is communicating with his direct reports plenty. Just not very well. Not only that, because he is communicating plenty, he is lulled into a false sense of security.

In fact, if this manager is like the vast majority, it is quite likely that the manager's communication is mostly ad hoc, hit or miss, surface level, and often pro forma. I call this "managing on autopilot."

The vast majority of managers do their "managing" more or less on autopilot until something goes wrong—and something always does. Then communication becomes more heated and urgent—sometimes even more accurate and effective. Managers almost always get most thoroughly involved when there are problems to address—large, medium, or small—what I've been referring to here as "firefighting."

Most managers think, "Everything is going just fine. It's just that we have a lot of fires to put out, and that makes it very hard to get into a good routine. Whenever you get into a good routine, pretty soon there is another fire." What they don't realize is that they are stuck in a vicious cycle:

> Managing on autopilot → False sense of security → Small problems have time to fester and grow → Problems inevitably blow up → Manager (and others) pulled into firefighting mode → Things get "back to normal," managing on autopilot.

How do you break the cycle?

In nearly every one of the thousands of cases I've studied, the solution is simple. Not easy. But simple. What's missing is almost always the fundamentals.

At RainmakerThinking, our research shows that very few (roughly one out of ten) managers are acing it. Too many are failing. The vast majority go through the motions, but not very well. This is what I call "undermanagement."

I've written extensively on the "undermanagement epidemic"— the widespread failure of leaders, managers, and supervisors to consistently practice Management 101 with excellence. For years, my focus has been on figuring out why. Why don't managers consistently practice the fundamentals with excellence?

Here's the thing: Most managers are trying. Most managers communicate plenty. And on the surface it often looks like they are practicing the fundamentals of Management 101. But in the vast majority of cases their management communication is severely lacking in both structure and substance. So the motions they are going through don't accomplish very much. And they don't realize it.

Practicing Management 101—just the fundamentals—requires discipline and rigor. It's not easy to maintain a high-structure, high-substance, ongoing one-on-one dialogue with every person you manage. Nonetheless, those are the fundamentals. If you are not doing that, how can you say in any meaningful way that you are "managing" someone?

If you are somebody's manager, then you have power over that person's livelihood and career, their ability to add value, and their ability to earn—this is how people put food on their table. They are working to make a living and take care of themselves and their families. And you are that person's boss. That is a profound responsibility. The least you can do is the fundamentals.

If the fundamentals are not working for you, then it is almost surely the case that you are not doing them right. The fundamentals are all you need. It's just that Management 101 is a more complex and difficult art than most people realize.

The Undermanagement Epidemic: Revisited

I've been conducting in-depth workplace research since 1993. Back then I was a frustrated young lawyer investigating the work attitudes of Generation X (those born between 1965 and 1977). That led to my first book, Managing Generation X, and quickly morphed into a career doing custom workplace research, consulting, and management training. From then on I've had a front-row seat from which to study workplace dynamics. I've spent most of my time interviewing, advising, and training managers at all levels: tens of thousands of managers, from CEOs to frontline supervisors, in just about every industry—retail, health care, research, finance, aerospace, software, manufacturing, the public sector, even nonprofits, you name it.

My company, RainmakerThinking, has been dedicated, since its founding, to conducting in-depth workplace research (ongoing surveys, questionnaires, strategic polls, focus groups, interviews, and literature review) to support this work. Over the years, our research has continually taken us back to the undermanagement epidemic.

Why?

Because undermanagement is almost always there, hiding in plain sight. It is so often what's going wrong in so many workplaces. It is rampant. It is costly. It is very easy to treat, but it is very hard to cure. The medicine is strong, so when you feel better, it's tempting to water it down. But as soon as you stop taking the strong medicine, you start to get sick again.

Our ongoing research shows that undermanagement is a perennial issue: The remarkably consistent data shows that nine out of ten managers fail to maintain an ongoing one-on-one dialogue sufficient to deliver on the "the fundamentals."

The costs and lost opportunities caused by undermanagement are incalculably high. How many tasks, responsibilities, and projects do managers do that could or should be delegated to someone else? If only the manager were managing closely enough to delegate properly. How many high performers leave their jobs because they don't have a good working relationship with their manager? How many low performers are hiding out, collecting a paycheck, because their manager is not keeping track? How many people would do more work or better work if they had more support, guidance, and direction from their manager? How many problems could be prevented or largely avoided or at least mitigated?

The solution: get managers to recognize that they are undermanaging and start practicing Management 101.

What has been thrilling to me (and our clients) has been the tremendous positive impact of back-to-fundamentals management. I've watched how just getting back to the fundamentals—learning and practicing the surprisingly complex art of Management 101—has dramatically improved the effectiveness—and the bottom-line results—of leaders and managers at all levels in organizations of all shapes and sizes. In the last two decades, I've taught the Surprisingly Difficult Art of Management 101 to hundreds of thousands of leaders and managers and supervisors. But not just to new managers or middle managers. I've also taught the same material to thousands of CEOs, CFOs, CIOs, COOs, four star Generals, other senior executives, even a few heads of state.

You never get so good (at anything) that you don't need to practice the fundamentals.

We've asked tens of thousands of nonmanagers over the last twenty years, "What is the one improvement you'd like to make in your relationship with your manager that would help you do your job better?" We ask this as an open-ended question. There are no multiple-choice options. Overwhelmingly, the most common response (from more than 60 percent of people)—far and away the number-one common denominator in responses, year after year—has been "communication." Usually "more communication" and/or "better communication."

We've asked tens of thousands of managers a similar question: "What is the one improvement you'd like to make in your relationships with your direct reports?" Again, the response is overwhelmingly (from more than 60 percent) "communication"—usually "more" and/or "better."

I always marvel at this, because in most workplaces there is an awful lot of communication. In most workplaces nowadays there are way too many emails, mediocre meetings, and lots of touching base, checking in, catching up, and just plain shooting the breeze. There's lots of communication in today's workplace. It's just mostly low-structure and low-substance. And so it's not accomplishing very much. That's why people crave "more" and "better" communication.

Here's the good news: The fundamentals work. The simple process of maintaining high-structure, high-substance, ongoing one-on-one dialogues really works wonders. When managers consistently practice this technique, employees get the guidance, direction, feedback, troubleshooting, and coaching they need. And the business results follow: increased employee performance and morale, increased retention of high performers, a necessary and welcome increase in turnover among low performers, and significant measurable improvements in business-outcomes. Not only that, but a steadily diminishing rate of management time spent "firefighting."

Here's the catch: It's not easy.

The first big hurdle for a manager who wants to get back to fundamentals and start practicing Management 101 is making the transition. Going from *not* maintaining high-structure, high-substance, ongoing one-on-one dialogues with every direct report to making them a regular practice is a big change. The manager needs to prepare for that change personally and professionally, then communicate this to colleagues and superiors, roll it out to direct reports, and then start doing it.

That's the second big hurdle: It's time-consuming, especially at first. Getting back to fundamentals usually requires a big up-front investment of extra time. If you haven't been doing it before, you will still have to fight all the fires you have not prevented at the same time you are investing time heavily in preventing future fires. You have to do double time for a while, until all the old fires die out. That's when you start getting your time back. But it takes a while. So you have to stick with it.

And that's the third big hurdle: Staying ahead of the cycle. In our research, managers tell us the biggest obstacle to consistently practicing the management fundamentals is that they simply don't have enough time. They have multiple competing priorities. There is always something more urgent than making sure to have those structured one-on-ones with their direct reports. Plus, there are so many meetings. On the other hand, managers say, they typically catch up with their direct reports in some of these meetings anyway, and they regularly touch base, check in, and are communicating throughout the day by phone and email and text. Not to mention, once in a while there is a true emergency—maybe an unavoidable emergency—that sucks everybody in and leaves everybody behind on everything. Then you really *don't* have time.

I've spent so much time behind the scenes in so many organizations that I can tell you this much: The managers who are most convinced that they don't have time to manage properly spend more time managing than any other managers. That is almost always the case.

The real problem is how they are spending their management time. These are nearly always the managers who spend an inordinate percentage of their management time "firefighting"—often solving problems that never had to happen in the first place or could have been identified and solved more easily at an earlier point. These are also nearly always the managers who spend surprisingly large amounts of time communicating with their direct reports in relatively low-structure, low-substance conversations, punctuated by way too many mediocre meetings.

Here's the really good news: When managers put their management time where it belongs—up front, every step of the way, before anything goes right, wrong, or average—the rigor and discipline does pay off. When managers consistently maintain the high-structure, high-substance, ongoing one-on-one dialogues, everything goes better. They get their time back.

Still, the hardest thing of all for most managers to do is really stick close to the fundamentals even when the heat is on. Our research shows that even the best managers are most likely to be thrown off their game by an acute crisis—even a relatively small one. Of course, nowadays you are always managing under pressure.

Why Managing People Is Hard

It's always been hard to manage people. It is much harder today than ever before, and it's getting harder every day.

Why?

Let's start with globalization and technology. The pace of change is accelerating for everyone all the time—from the macro level all the way down to the micro. In today's knowledge-driven, machine-powered, highly interconnected, fiercely competitive global marketplace, everything is complex, fast-moving, and always in flux. Work that used to take weeks must be done in moments. Relationships that would have been nearly impossible due to geography are now taken for granted. Communication and travel are nearly instantaneous.

Yet we are also vulnerable in entirely new ways. One technical glitch today can slow down (or shut down) your operation for days or weeks at a time—not just in your own machines, but in machines who-knows-where with which you had no idea you had any connection whatsoever. An earthquake on the other side of the world today— actual or metaphorical—could affect you today in ways you probably cannot even imagine, including ways that didn't exist yesterday. Not to mention your customers, vendors, contractors, partners, colleagues, and counterparts in other departments and workgroups.

Everybody is under more pressure. The corporate order of the day is to run ever more lean and flexible. Squeeze more and more productivity and quality out of tightly controlled resources. Chase innovation and technology to keep from falling behind. Manage talent as a capital (depreciating) asset, in the wake of a profound transformation in the fundamental employer-employee relationship. After decades of constant downsizing, restructuring, and reengineering, nobody expects to pay their dues and climb the corporate ladder anymore.

Job security has been dead for some time now. The default presumption of long-term hierarchical employment relationships has been replaced by a new presumptive career path built on a growing portfolio of short-term transactional employment relationships of varying scope and duration.

Never forget that most employees work because they must. They work to support themselves and their families. Most are pursuing some kind of intermediate and longer-term security, but today that plan is rarely contingent on a long-term relationship with one particular employer. Very few employees now look at one employer as a primary source of their long-term career security, much less their long-term economic security.

The problem is that the promise (implied or even explicit) of long-term vesting rewards from employers is no longer enough to get employees to perform today. Employees are less willing to follow orders, work harder, and contribute their best today in exchange for vague promises about what they might get in five years or ten years. Who knows where they'll be in five or ten years?! There is simply too much uncertainty.

Employees today want to know, "What do you want from me today, tomorrow, this week, this month, this year? And what do you have to offer me in return today, tomorrow, this week, this month, this year?"

Managers today are always in danger of losing good people. People come and go. People move around internally. These factors militate against continuity in working relationships. Sometimes those who are least likely to leave are the hardest to manage. Everybody is a special case.

Managing people has become an ongoing (sometimes daily) negotiation. That is high maintenance!

At the same time, most managers, like most everybody else, are being asked to do more with less. They have more of their own non-management tasks and responsibilities, increased administrative burdens and growing managerial spans of control, often including employees working in different locations or on different schedules, as well as depending more and more on people in other workgroups and departments. With so much resource and process streamlining, there is growing interdependency in almost everybody's work. Everything we do now involves a lot of moving parts. We depend on so many other people, all the time.

Meanwhile, as always, everybody involved is human. People have feelings. That's a significant consideration for everybody involved.

There are so many factors beyond any one manager's control. Maybe it feels like our problems have outgrown the fundamentals. Our situation is too complex. Our challenges are too advanced. Most managers simply convince themselves that the fundamentals are simply no longer enough, or they just don't have time.

How Most Managers Spend Most
of Their Management Time

Let's go back to the manager of Project Q at the beginning of this chapter. If you interviewed a manager like this one privately (as I do all the time in my research), asking him how he had managed the project, he would say something like this:

> Listen, I already spend tons of time communicating with my direct reports, not to mention my various bosses, and counterparts in other workgroups and other departments. Look at Project Q. I was holding regular team meetings. On top of the multitude of other meetings I must attend on and off all day long, every day. I touch base with everybody every day. I have an open door policy. If anything comes up, we let each other know as needed. Plus we talk and email with each other all day long. Until everything fell apart, everything was going just fine.

Indeed, this is what managers tell us in our interviews and seminars, with striking consistency. Most managers spend the vast majority of their management time on four pernicious time drains:

#1. Attending Too Many Mediocre Group Meetings

Group meetings, team meetings, cross-functional teams, special projects, committees. Meetings are the number one time suck for managers. Ask any manager.

Most of us work in highly interdependent workplaces where we all must rely on each other on complex projects with lots of moving pieces. With more and more people working interdependently, there are more and more meetings.

At its best, a meeting is great for:

- Communicating in-person information that everybody needs to know
- When multiple people need to discuss and solve a problem together
- Shared experience to build cohesion, commitment, and motivation

But so many meetings are not very good at all. Too many people attend too many meetings in which they neither add value nor take anything valuable away. Five people in a room for an hour—that's five hours of productive capacity in that room. You better make those meetings good.

Meetings are also not very good for creating real accountability. It's too easy to hide in a team meeting. It's even easier to point fingers and divert attention.

#2. Wading Through a Never-Ending Tidal Wave of Email

Electronic communication is at everybody's fingertips all the time. Your inbox pulls you in and demands you reply. It's so hard to resist.

At its best, email is great for:

- Communicating remotely information that everybody needs to know
- Documenting verbal communication
- Maintaining asynchronous conversations in between scheduled conversations

But so much of email is unnecessary, duplicative, and/or sloppy. The most pernicious thing about all that email is that mixed in with all the bad email is important information, and we want to assume that, because we sent it, the recipient has read and understood it. Even worse than a message never sent is a message sent but never received.

#3. Touching Base, Checking In, and Shooting the Breeze

"How are you?" "How's everything going?" "Is everything on track?" "Are there any problems I should know about?"

These are the questions managers most commonly ask their direct reports, yet they tell you so little about what's really going on. They are gestures, mostly. You might as well say, "Tell me you are fine." "Tell me everything is going fine." "Tell me everything is on track." "Tell me there are no problems I should know about."

The worst thing about management by "touching base" is that it makes you feel like you are staying on top of things, but it takes a lot more than rhetorical questions to really stay on top.

The right questions are: "What did you do? How did you do it? What steps did you take? What step are you on right now? Let me see what you've got so far. What are you going to do next? How are you going to do it? What steps are you going to follow? How long will each step take?" Questions like that can't be asked and answered in a meaningful way if the conversation happens just in passing.

#4. Interrupting and Being Interrupted

Something pops into your head, you interrupt them. Something pops into their head, they interrupt you. "Do you have a minute?"

When you are interrupted, you are not at your best. Most likely you were in the middle of something. You have to break your attention. Pull yourself out of whatever it is you were doing. Try to focus. But you are not prepared. And what you really want is to get back to whatever it is you were doing before you were interrupted. Your responses to your direct reports (and anyone else) when you are interrupted are never going to be as thorough and accurate as they would be if you had time to prepare.

The same is true for your direct reports and other colleagues when you interrupt them.

Formal Reviews Are Not Enough

Beyond these four common time drains, most managers also are required to spend a certain amount of time and energy on periodic formal reviews. Depending on the organization, it may be a yearly ritual or it may be much more often. In any event, these formal reviews often take up a lot of time and attention.

What often passes for structured or substantive management communication—sometimes the only such communication—are the performance reviews that managers are required by most organizations to have with their direct reports annually or every six months or every quarter. Three, six, and twelve month reviews have long been notorious for their lack of efficacy. Employees have told us for years in our interviews that formal reviews rarely give them meaningful, helpful feedback:

"They do it just because they have to."

"Sometimes they don't even do it."

"They do it late or last minute."

"Some managers just ask the employees to write their own reviews."

"It's all politics, who they like."

"Reviews are too vague."

"Reviews are too specific, mentioning something that happened months and months ago."

"My review was done by someone who doesn't even manage me day to day."

"My review focused on things I can't control like overall numbers that are not just affected by my performance."

And so on.

In general, formal reviews tend to fall somewhere on the spectrum between two extremes. On one end they focus on highly subjective feedback but without the benefit of regular, ongoing, day-to-day feedback along the way. This sort of review tends to be idiosyncratic and incidental, reflecting what a manager has observed, if there is a big win or if there is a notable problem.

More and more common is the other end of the spectrum, in which reviews increasingly rely on the elements of employee performance that are tracked (more or less) automatically—bottom-line numbers that appear in weekly or monthly reports. Managers at all levels today are given performance objectives (usually articulated in numbers) for every dimension of their operations. The very worthy intention is to place the focus on concrete, measurable outcomes. The problem is that usually the numbers serve as a trigger for cascading recrimination (or praise), even though what gets measured is often not tied directly to actions in the control of individual employees. Meanwhile, most leading organizations are moving to some form of "forced ranking." This is the practice whereby managers are required to make candid evaluations of every employee according to a tightly proscribed distribution of grades such as A, B, and C. Sadly, although evaluation and differentiation are key, this is an exercise in annual guesswork unless managers are monitoring, measuring, and documenting every employee's performance on an ongoing basis. Once, twice, or four times a year doesn't do the trick. When the manager does not monitor and measure and document each employee's actual performance (concrete actions within his or her control) on an ongoing basis, ranking—and the differential rewards that go with ranking—often are not clearly enough connected to the performance of each individual in question. So the system is perceived as capricious and unfair. Over and over again, I have seen forced-ranking and pay-for-performance initiatives result in disastrous morale because managers failed to do the necessary work.

The Inevitable Challenges Every Manager Must Face with Surprising Regularity

If you were still interviewing the manager of Project Q, this time asking him to do a postmortem on exactly what went wrong, if he is like most of the managers we've studied, he'd probably say something like this:

> As usual, the problems that occurred were due to a bunch of
> factors beyond my control. We lost our best employee, and
> her replacement was not yet up to speed. Resources are tight.
> There were changes in the project specifications that came from

someone else somewhere else—maybe a customer or a vendor
or a counterpart in another group in another department. That
change was not fully communicated to the right people. There
were a lot of moving pieces. And somebody dropped the ball.
We are understaffed. Or wrongly staffed. Some people refuse to
pull their weight.

I'm doing the best I can under the circumstances. Things
were going just fine. Until everything fell apart. All due to factors beyond my control.

Managers tell us this every day. Most of the firefighting (not to
mention all the false alarms) seems unavoidable, yet our research shows
that the most frequently occurring problems come up over and over
again. The overwhelming majority of the seemingly inevitable problems that vex managers almost always flow from these factors:

• **Personnel discontinuity.** People come and go. That's always
been true. But employment relationships today are far more short-
term and fluid than they have been before in the modern economy.
So you are always losing good people. And you are always trying to
get new people on board and up to speed. On top of that, one great
employee is worth more than three or four or five mediocre employees. Sometimes you have to go to great lengths to effectively reward,
retain, and develop the very best employees.

• **Constant change coming at you from every direction.**
Technology. The markets. The weather. Geopolitics. Micropolitics.
Customer requirements; vendor requirements; employee requirements. Change regularly forces rework, often involving lots of
moving parts, and therefore lots of counterparts here, there, and
everywhere.

• **Interdependency.** Again, more and more of our work involves
lots of moving parts and therefore lots of counterparts here, there, and
everywhere. Most people must rely on many others within and outside
of their immediate work group in order to do their own work.

- **Resource constraints**. Nowadays everybody is expected to do more with less. Increasingly, people report that they are making do with tighter resources and longer and more complex supply lines with shorter lead times. Often people find themselves trying to do their jobs with what they feel are insufficient resources.

- **Employees being human**. Human beings have weaknesses as well as strengths. Humans are not always great at self-management. They have habits, and not always good ones. Not only that, but everybody has bad days. Some people have bad weeks, months, and years. Productivity and quality of work are highly variable, sometimes due to employee performance. On top of all that, humans have attitudes, and not always good ones.

So what's a manager to do? What do the very best managers do?

For many years, in the research we conduct before, during, and after our management seminars, we have studied what the very best managers actually do that is different from the others. I'm talking about the very best managers: managers whose employees consistently deliver the highest productivity and quality, with high retention of high performers and high turnover among low performers, with the best business outcomes and high morale and team spirit, whose direct reports are most likely to describe the manager as "one of the best managers I've ever had." What is the common denominator among those managers? An abiding commitment to the fundamentals—relentless high-quality communication. Consistently engaging every direct report in an ongoing, highly structured, content-rich one-on-one dialogue about the work that needs to be done by that person. Things go much better when managers consistently make expectations clear and provide candid feedback for every individual every step of the way. Use team meetings only for what team meetings are good for—and make the most of them.

When managers build and maintain high-quality one-on-one dialogues with their direct reports, they almost always increase employee performance and morale, increase retention of high performers and turnover among low performers, and achieve significant measurable improvements in business outcomes.

Here's the really good news: They spend less and less time firefighting. They get ahead of the problems and prevent the fires. They break the vicious cycle. They start getting their management time back. Then, if they don't slip up on the fundamentals, a virtuous upward spiral begins to build.

How do you break free from the vicious cycle? Those regular one-on-ones are your fire prevention, preparation, and training. That's where real impact occurs. Not in the crucial conversations, but rather in the routine conversations. First you need to make those routine conversations much, much better.

How to Make Those Routine Conversations Much, Much Better: High Structure, High Substance

As a manager, do you want to stop agonizing? Do you want to stop struggling? Do you want to sidestep one crisis after another? Do you want to get the most out of your people? Do you want to quickly master the seemingly most difficult management relationships?

I teach managers to do what the very best managers do: Build and maintain an ongoing, regular one-on-one dialogue with every person you manage in order to:

- Make expectations clear
- Track performance and provide ongoing candid feedback
- Provide support, direction, troubleshooting, and guidance
- Make accountability a process, not a slogan
- Recognize and reward in line with performance

That's it. Highly structured, highly substantive one-on-one dialogue. Of course, there is much nuance in the details.

What Is High Structure?

High structure means regularly scheduled and conducted according to a clear, well-organized agenda. That doesn't mean it should be a one-way conversation. Of course, you need to allow for give and take.

The first person you need to manage every day is yourself. You need to set aside the time every day to manage. I recommend a minimum of an hour a day; think of it as like taking a walk every day. Make that your sacrosanct time for managing. During that hour, do not fight fires. Use that hour for managing up front, before anything goes right, wrong, or average.

The second person you need to manage every day is everybody else. In an ideal world, you would talk with every single direct report every single day. You would take that management walk every day with every person. However, if you have more than four or five direct reports, you will need to make choices every day. Maybe you can't talk to every person every day.

For your dedicated one-on-one time:

- Set aside an hour a day.
- Concentrate on three or four people per day.
- Prepare in advance and make sure your direct reports prepare too.
- Follow a regular format with each person, customized for that person.
- Always start with top priorities, open questions, and any work in progress.
- Consider holding these conversations standing up, with a clipboard in hand (to keep them quick and focused).
- Don't do all the talking.
- Don't let anybody go more than two weeks without getting together.
- If you manage people who work other shifts, stay late or come in early.

- If you manage people in remote locations, conduct your one-on-ones via telephone with no less rigor and discipline than your in-person one-on-ones.

How many people can you possibly manage this way? How many one-on-one dialogues can you maintain? The answer is different for every manager. Be honest with yourself. If you are not able to maintain an ongoing one-on-one dialogue with an employee, you are not managing that person. That person is in a sink-or-swim situation. If you have eight people, you can talk to everybody one-on-one once or twice a week. If you have sixteen people, it's going to be a whole lot harder.

If you have a chain of command, use it. Focus first and foremost on any managers you manage. Talk with them about how they are managing. Every day, coach them on the management fundamentals—make sure they are having regular one-on-ones with their direct reports. All the way down the chain of command. Managers need to be taught to practice the fundamentals at every level. If you don't, your chain of command is not going to work.

No matter how many people you are responsible for managing, you have to make choices every day about how you are going to use your management time.

What Is High Substance?

High substance means rich in immediately relevant content, specific to the person and the situation, with a clear execution focus.

Talk about what's going right, wrong, and average. What needs to be done? What are the next steps? And the next steps after that? Spell out expectations in clear and vivid terms, every step of the way:

- Remind each person of broad performance standards regularly.
- Turn best practices into standard operating procedures and teach them to everybody.
- Use plans and step-by-step checklists whenever possible.

- Focus on concrete actions within the control of the individual employee.
- Monitor, measure, and document individual performance in writing.
- Follow up, follow up, follow up, and provide regular, candid, coaching-style feedback.
- Follow through with real consequences and rewards based on performance in relation to expectations.

Ask really good questions:
- "What do you need from me?"
- "What is your plan? What steps will you follow?"
- "How long will this step take? How long will that step take? And the next?"

Listen carefully:
- Evaluate how well the employee understands the requirements of the task at hand.
- Pay close attention to the gaps in her approach.
- Keep asking questions. Facilitate.
- Adjust as needed.
- Never forget, you need to make sure every single employee knows every step of the way exactly what is expected of her—exactly what she is supposed to do and how.

One-on-ones are also where you answer employees' questions as they come up. Get input from your employees throughout the process. Learn from what your employees are learning on the front line. Strategize together. Provide advice, support, motivation, and even inspiration once in a while. Together you'll need to regularly think through potential obstacles and pitfalls—make back-up planning part of every work plan. Anticipate and prepare. Train and practice.

Together you will uncover on a regular basis what can be done and what cannot, what resources are necessary, what problems may occur, what expectations are reasonable, what goals and deadlines are sufficiently ambitious, and what counts as success versus failure.

Every step of the way, stay on the lookout: Are there problems hiding around the corner or just below the surface? Small problems that can be solved now so they don't turn into bigger problems soon? Resources we need to obtain or else figure out what to do instead? Key people in interdependent roles we need to be engaging?

What's changing? What's about to change? What might change soon? Don't be embarrassed that things change. It wasn't your idea. Uncertainty is the new certainty, right? When priorities change, expectations change. That is just further evidence that telling people what to do and how to do it is critical. After all, no one else is going to tell each employee:

- Which priorities have shifted and changed today
- What they are supposed to focus on today
- What the expectations are today

That's it. That's how you break free from the vicious cycle. It's all about making those routine conversations much, much better. It's just the fundamentals—practiced consistently with rigor and discipline.

The People List

No matter how consistently you practice the discipline of the one-on-one dialogues, you will quickly find that you need to customize your approach with every person. Every employee is different. What works with one person may not work with another. Every employee presents unique needs and expectations and corresponding challenges for the manager.

I spend a lot of time helping managers figure out how to customize their approach to each person. The one-on-one dialogue you build with one employee will be very different from the one-on-one dialogue you build with another: why you are talking, what you are talking about, how you talk, where you talk, when, and how often.

In the later stages of my advanced seminars, I teach managers how to use a tool I call the "People List." This is a running list of all the key people with whom you need to be engaged in a one-on-one dialogue right now. Maybe it includes your boss or your bosses, peers, and counterparts in other groups or departments, internally and externally. But first and foremost, your People List should include your direct reports, always. Anybody who considers you his boss deserves a place on your People List, so long as that person reports to you.

You should definitely start keeping a People List. Why not start it right now? Who are all the key people with whom you need to be engaged in a one-on-one dialogue right now? Your boss? Key peers and counterparts? Definitely your direct reports at the very least.

1. Make the list; actually, make a simple spreadsheet. Write (or type) the names in a far left column of the page.
2. To the right of each name, make a note: When and where was your last conversation with that person? Regarding what?
3. Now give that last conversation a grade for structure and substance. Would you give it an A+? B? C?
4. In the next column, answer this question for each person: What should you be talking about with this person? When and where are you going to have your next conversation? And what do you need to do to prepare in advance?

That's your People List.

You should be asking and answering those questions for yourself every day until you get into the habit of the one-on-ones. Once you are really, really in the habit, your People List will change. How you use it will evolve to meet your needs. But never stop asking and answering those questions. Never stop keeping your People List. You never outgrow the fundamentals. No matter how rigorous and disciplined your routine, no matter how advanced your management skills may become, you can always benefit from asking and answering those questions for yourself every day. Your People List will keep you closely moored to the fundamentals and keep you from slipping away.

There's No Such Thing as Advanced Management

In our advanced management seminars, I take experienced managers through one problem-solving session after another. We focus on one real life case study after another—the real employees the managers are really managing in the real world. "Who are the employees with whom you are really struggling? What are the really tough cases?"

Of course, like clockwork, the same basic cases come up over and over again—the same 27. Maybe it's the superstar whom the manager is afraid of losing, the slacker whom the manager cannot figure out how to motivate, the one with an attitude problem, or the two who cannot get along. From tracking managers before, during, and after the training, I've identified the most frequently occurring "most difficult challenges" with which managers tend to struggle and the best step-by-step solutions.

Of course, I've learned through our years of research and training that different challenges yield most readily to specially focused techniques. What's astounding, however, is how (nearly) every challenge—even the most difficult—yields to the healing, powerful, vanquishing medicine of relentless high-quality communication.

Throughout this book, I show you how to apply the management fundamentals to the 27 challenges managers most often face. Again, the 27 challenges are not enumerated in order of frequency or difficulty. Rather, I've grouped the most frequent challenges into chapters based on the larger issues they have in common:

- Leadership transitions; being the "new" manager
- Employee self-management; work habits
- Performance management

- Employee attitudes
- Managing superstar employees
- Managing despite factors beyond your control
- The need for a fresh start to an old relationship; renewal

In each chapter I examine the underlying theme and show how, almost always, the ad hoc manner in which most managers talk to their direct reports every day actually leads inevitably to the most difficult employee situations that tend to vex managers. What is the key to avoiding most of these problems and the key to solving them quickly and with relative ease as soon as they appear? High-structure, high-substance one-on-one dialogues with every direct report. With each of the most common challenges managers face within each area, I show how managers typically respond to these problems when they become aware and how these typical responses sometimes exacerbate the problems. Then I explain how to use the structured dialogue to control the situation and zero in on the specially focused techniques for continuing to grow the one-on-one dialogue in this situation.

The fundamentals are all you need.

CHAPTER TWO

The Challenges of Being the "New" Manager

You are the new leader. Congratulations! On day one, you have two critical missions:

- Establish yourself as a strong, highly engaged leader.
- Learn who's who and what's what.

Take note: you'll have to pursue those two missions simultaneously, right out of the gate. Ready, set, go!

Leadership transitions occur every day in the workplace, at all levels, in organizations of every shape and size. In today's fast-moving world, leaders come and go and come back again. That's why we so often take these transitions for granted, gloss over them, and miss tremendous opportunities in the process.

Even in a fluid work environment, if you are my new manager, that has profound implications, at least for me! If you are my new boss, all of a sudden you are the person upon whom I will rely more than any other individual for meeting my basic needs and expectations at work. You will be my go-to person for dealing with just about any issue that arises at work. You will be my point of contact, but much more than that: on a daily basis you will have a huge defining impact on my day-to-day work experience. If you are the boss, it is your responsibility to make sure everything goes well. Employees look to you first when they need something, when they want something, or when something is going wrong. If there's a problem, you are the solution.

If you are going to be my new manager, the first thing I want to know is: What kind of manager are you going to be?

That's one of the great things about being a manager who is committed to the fundamentals. How can anyone object to a manager who says, "I'm going to be strong and highly engaged"? Would you rather your manager be weak and hands-off?

One would think that it would be safe for a manager to say:

I'm your new manager, and I consider that a sacred responsibility. I'm going to make sure that everything goes well around here. I'm going to help you get a bunch of work done very well, very fast, all day long. I'm going to set you up for success every step of the way. I'm going to spell out expectations for you and help you plan. I'm going to work with you to clarify goals, guidelines, and specifications. I'm going to help you break big deadlines into smaller time frames with concrete performance benchmarks. I'm going to go over standard operating procedures. I'm going to offer reminders. I'm going to provide checklists and other tools. I'm going to help you keep track of what you are doing and how you are doing it every step of the way. I'm going to help you monitor and measure and document your success every step of the way. I'm going to help you solve problems as soon as they occur, so they don't fester and grow into bigger problems. I'm going to help you find the shortcuts, avoid the pitfalls, and follow the best practices. Count on me. When you need something, I'm going to help you find it. When you want something, I'm going to help you earn it.

That's what I call the "Good news!" management speech. That's a very good message to deliver in your inaugural team meeting.

You would think that most people would take that as good news. But remember, many workplaces are still caught in the grip of the undermanagement epidemic. Be prepared. Ask yourself: Does the culture support strong management? Or is everybody else around here pretty hands-off? What will it mean for you, in the context of this corporate culture, to become a very strong, highly engaged, transactional, coaching-style boss? Will you fit right in? Or will this make you something of a stand-out—and not in a good way?

Sometimes managers tell me:

"This organization is very conservative. We don't believe in confrontation."

"This organization is very progressive. We don't like to boss people around."

"Our organization is very large, and there is lots of red tape and bureaucracy."

"Our organization is very small, and there is more of a family dynamic in the workplace."

"Our work is very technical."

"Our work is very creative."

"Our employees are much older."

"Our employees are much younger."

"Our employees do low-level grunt work."

"Our employees are all high-level professionals."

Good news! In every case, the fundamentals are still the fundamentals. What can you do about it? Be different. And don't keep it a secret: stand out as the manager who is serious about the work and managing. If being strong makes you stand out, then stand out. You may find out that the culture supports good management after all. There may be more hands-on managers in your midst than you realize, doing their thing beneath the radar. Or you may find that your example is an inspiration to others.

Start by introducing yourself and establishing yourself as a leader. You need to assume command: "This is who I am as a manager. This is how I operate. This is how I'm going to manage."

Then what?

The big challenge for you as a brand-new leader is that, no matter how much experience you may bring to the table, you are brand new to this particular role. You have a huge learning curve to climb. You need to learn your new job, which can mean relearning everything you already know from a whole new perspective. You need to learn a whole new cast of characters. You need to learn the job of every one of your new direct reports. On top of all that, if you are new to the organization or the industry even, you have entire layers of extra learning on top of the job-specific and team-specific learning. That's a lot of learning.

I've seen so many new managers—and plenty of experienced ones—daunted by the learning curve in a new leadership role and thus hesitant to assume command decisively at the outset. One such leader, a new manager in an agricultural company (I'll call him "Aggie"), told me, "I figured, 'I'm new around here. They've been doing their thing for a long time.' I made a point to lay low for the first couple of months while I was really learning the job. There were plenty of meetings, and I was introduced as the manager, and I was in charge, for all intents and purposes. But to be honest, it was pretty clear that I had a lot to learn about the company, not to mention the team. I was taking over an experienced team. They were all talking over my head in the first meetings. They had ongoing work to do. I figured I should learn first, then take charge later."

How did that work out?

Aggie said: "It didn't work well at all. As I started to learn what was going on, getting up to speed a little, I started asking more and more questions. I started getting more in their business. There was a lot of resistance at first. They were giving me some attitude. Like it was none of my business what they were doing. It took me a long time to win their respect. I'm not sure I ever recovered from that weak start."

Regardless of your particular onboarding schedule as a new leader, you can be sure of this: On day one, the introduction, orientation, onboarding, and up-to-speed learning around your new management relationships will start happening. The only question is this: Are you going to make sure you have a high-structure, high-substance process from the start, or not? When the first days and weeks of your new management relationship are not well planned, coordinated, and carried out, new working relationships get off on a much weaker footing, and sometimes they never recover. There is no opportunity to clearly establish the basic terms of the relationship: who's who and what's what, the ground rules, the broad performance standards, and the basic guidelines for how team members are going to communicate on a regular basis. As a result, you get plenty of surprises and misunderstandings. It is nearly impossible to measure the cascading effects of such a weak start.

Who can afford a weak start?

Where Aggie went wrong was in assuming that being in a learning mode was somehow inconsistent with asserting himself as a strong new leader of the team. His big mistake was assuming that having a lot to learn is a position of vulnerability. Of course, the irony is that you don't really start learning what you need to learn until you actually take charge and dig into the details. Aggie realized: "When I thought I was up to speed, I started asking a lot of questions. But it wasn't until I started asking those questions that I was truly getting up to speed in any meaningful way. Those were the questions I should have started with on day one.

"I've learned a big lesson: When you are new, you have such awareness of all that you have to learn. This is not a position of weakness. It is a position of strength. I wish I had come in on day one and said to the team: 'This is who I am. This is how I'm going to manage. My first mission is to learn everything, inside out, and that is how we are going to become acquainted. Each of you is going to teach me.'"

The fact that your first mission is to learn doesn't have to change that dynamic one bit. The best way to end your inaugural team meeting (where you deliver your "Good news!" management speech) is to schedule your first one-on-ones with every person on the team. Learning is your position of strength. From day one, stake it out and use it. The first order of business is, you need to get introduced to everyone and everything. You need to get on board and up to speed with everyone and everything by learning the nuts and bolts of their jobs from day one. You don't learn first and take charge later.

You take charge by learning, in these ways and more:

- **In every one-on-one conversation with every employee, ask pointed questions:** "What do you do? How do you do it?" Then move on to discuss next steps. "What are you going to do next? How? How long is that going to take? Why?" Then follow up next time. "What did you do? How did you do it?"

- **Watch employees work.** You learn a lot from actually watching someone performing his tasks and responsibilities in action that you cannot learn any other way.

- **Ask employees to help you keep track of their actions** by using self-monitoring tools like project plans, checklists, and activity logs. Employees can monitor whether they are meeting goals and deadlines laid out in a project plan, make notations on checklists, and report to you at regular intervals. Activity logs are diaries that employees can keep, noting exactly what they do all day, including breaks and interruptions. Each time the employee moves on to a new activity, he is asked to note the time and the new activity he is turning to. Of course, an activity log can become overly granular and burdensome if it is completed down to the minute. Still, it's a huge reality check for anyone to complete a comprehensive activity log (at least for a week or so). As an ongoing process, it's probably wise to encourage employees to keep activity logs in reasonable increments of time—maybe in fifteen-minute (or thirty-minute) chunks.

- **Check your employees' work carefully in process.** If an employee is not responsible for producing a tangible end product, then watching that employee work is the same thing as reviewing work in progress. If she is responsible for an end product, spot-check it while she is working on it. You can't actually keep track of everything every employee does, but you can check random samples on a regular basis.

- **Gather intelligence.** Ask customers, vendors, coworkers, and other managers about their interactions with specific employees. Always ask questions about the employee's *work*, never about the person. Don't ask for evaluations; ask for descriptions. Don't ask for impressions; ask for details. And don't believe everything you hear; the unverified statements of third parties are simply hearsay. But the more you keep your ear to the ground, the more you know which sources can be trusted. So ask around on a regular basis.

One employee at a time, one day at a time, you will become the person who knows the most about who is doing what, where, when, why, and how, every step of the way. The more knowledge you acquire, the more power you'll have. When do you finish learning and start running the show? Never! Managing is always one part learning and one part teaching. If you ever stop learning, you should not be running the show anymore.

Start Strong!

Start out being intensely hands-on with each person, so you can figure out quickly exactly how closely each person needs to be managed. You will need to calibrate and recalibrate your management approach with each individual.

Let your direct reports know that they have a huge amount of power in helping you recalibrate: demonstrating consistently high productivity, high quality, and great attitude is the way to gain increased responsibility and less frequent one-on-ones. Mastery is the key to autonomy: alert the employee that you have high expectations, and as she delivers on those expectations, you can gradually back off. If an employee's performance falters in any way, tighten the reins for a while.

By the time you are eight to ten weeks into a new management role (or relationship), the nuances of your management challenge will become increasingly clear. You will have a better idea of who is doing what, where, when, why, and how. You've had plenty of surprises, and probably by now you are getting over them. It is likely you've done some adjusting along the way. Your meetings with each person will start to feel like standard operating procedure. If you've been monitoring, measuring, and documenting each person's performance in your tracking system, then you will have accumulated a written record of patterns for each person.

Once you've had a chance to digest what's going on and have given your new management relationships a chance to take hold, you will naturally get to a point where some decisions are obvious. You need to fire one person. Another you want to make darned sure not to lose. Perhaps you realize that it would be wise to shift around certain tasks and responsibilities from one person to another. You realize you need to meet with one employee every day, but others only once or twice a week.

Whatever those decisions may be, trust what you are learning through the process. Stay flexible every step of the way. Be prepared to revise and adjust as you keep learning, and as circumstances and people change—as they inevitably do. No matter what, don't stop meeting regularly with every person. Keep monitoring and measuring and documenting.

Continue asking yourself:

- Who needs to be managed more closely?
- Who needs more responsibility and autonomy?
- Who needs help navigating the complex, ever-changing workplace?
- Who needs help with the fundamentals of self-management?
- Who needs performance coaching to speed up or slow down?
- Who has a great attitude, and who needs an attitude adjustment?
- Who is likely to improve? Who is not?
- Who should be developed? Who should be fired?
- Who are your best people? Who are your real performance problems?
- Who requires special accommodations and rewards? Who deserves them?

MANAGEMENT CHALLENGE #1:
WHEN GOING FROM PEER TO LEADER

You finally got the promotion. Congratulations! Yesterday you were a team member. Today you are in charge of that same team.

When you are promoted from within, you can easily make the mistake of thinking you already know everything and everyone. You already have relationships with everyone, and you likely already have strong opinions about who's who and what's what.

Guess what? They already have opinions about you too. Those who were your peers just the day before are your direct reports today. That may include some people with more experience than you; some who think that they, not you, should have received the promotion; people with whom you didn't get along beforehand; people with whom you got along just fine; and people who were your "work friends" at work only, or those who are your social friends outside of work as well.

Now you are their former peer and their brand-new boss. All of a sudden you have power and influence in relation to their careers and livelihoods and their ability to do valuable work that is recognized and rewarded. You are also now the primary link between those individuals and the next level of leadership—you represent the organization as an employer. For your direct reports, you are the key to helping them get the resources they need to succeed, getting approvals, removing obstacles, and facilitating their interactions with lateral counterparts.

That is a huge shift, and it will radically change your relationships with everybody at work. If it doesn't seem to change your relationships, then something else is very likely going terribly wrong beneath the surface. Power changes relationships. That change must be handled with integrity and transparency, with diligence and rigor, with structure and substance.

So often I've seen new managers in this situation try to soft-pedal their new authority: "Don't think of me as your boss. I'm still just me. We work together. I'm just one of the team." That is, until there's a disagreement, or an unpopular decision needs to be made or a new policy implemented, or someone needs to be held accountable or needs to be called out for special recognition and reward. Because all of that will now fall to you.

I always tell new managers in this situation, "Remember, you are the one who got the promotion. Live up to it." You must own it. I learned this from a young mechanical contractor who was running a team he had worked on for several years. He told me, "You can't let them make you feel bad about being the boss. The guys would say stuff like 'Hey Sam. You used to be in this position. You should know where we are coming from.' And I'd say, 'I was in your position, but you've never been in my position. So remember, I do understand your perspective, because I've been there, but I have other factors I need to consider now that I am in this position. Please respect that.' I have been in that position, so I really do try to take that perspective into account. My job is to help everybody do a better job and have an easier time of it."

When you get that promotion and all of sudden you are the new manager of your old team, you have two choices: behave in such a way that your former peers wonder why you are the new boss instead of one of them, or else do such a good job that nobody will ever wonder.

What About When Some of Your New Direct Reports Are Actually Your Friends?

If you are taking over a team on which you have been a member, it is very likely that you may have formed some friendships in the course of working together. Sometimes the friendship even predates the working relationship. Either way, it can be hard to separate your role as the new boss from your role as friend. But that's exactly what you have to do. As tempting as it might be to pretend you are still just a member of the team, still one of the guys, you have to accept that you are in a different role now.

1. **Decide which is more important to you.** If the friendship is more important, maybe you shouldn't be the boss. Accept the fact that your role as boss might compromise or damage the friendship.

Maybe you'll decide that you cannot risk your friendship and thus you don't want to be the boss. But probably not.

2. **Establish ground rules that keep the roles separate.** Say: "Our friendship is very important to me. My job is also very important to me, and around here I am the boss. When we are at work, I need to be the boss. When we are outside work, we try to leave that behind."

3. **Be a good manager.** Protect the friendship by making sure things go really well at work. Minimize the number of problems, and you will minimize the number of potential conflicts in your personal relationship.

4. **Accept that the parameters of your friendship have changed.** Recognize and embrace the fact that the work you and your friend have in common will become more and more the terrain of your friendship. That's OK. With any luck, you will both find the work you share to be interesting and important.

As much as you try to keep work separate from your friendship and your friendship separate from your work, the boundaries won't always be clear. Take good care of your friendship by being a diligent, thorough manager, and hope that your friend will do the same by helping you do that to the best of your ability.

Coming on Too Strong

Next to soft-pedaling authority, the most common mistake made by new managers promoted from within the team is coming on too strong. Sometimes when you are promoted from within you may feel like you need to prove yourself right away. Assert strength and confidence. Take on any detractors. Show them who is boss now! Or maybe you have been eager to take charge for so long that you are sure you know what's what, who's who, and what needs to be done. I remember one such manager very well. I had been working closely with the finance department of a large scientific research company and was watching one rising star (I'll call her "Ms. Finance") very closely, because I knew she was going to be promoted soon. I knew Ms. Finance had a lot of opinions about how the finance operation could be improved. Sure enough, on her first day as manager, she pulled together the fourteen-member team of accountants and financial analysts into a conference room and made the following statement: "I've been waiting for this day for a long time. Things are going to change. There will be no more of the standard BS on my watch! I'm going to hold everybody's feet to the fire. If you want something from me, you had better be prepared to earn it! Any questions?"

There was a minor insurrection. Ms. Finance later told me: "It took me a while to [undo the damage]. I had a lot of unwinding to do." Not only that, but of course, Ms. Finance quickly discovered that everything and everyone was *not* exactly as they had seemed to her from her vantage point as a team member. Ms. Finance quickly began to realize that things look quite different from the manager's vantage point:

> I could see that some people I had really underestimated. People I thought were not that valuable were doing a lot of really important work. I just had had no visibility into that. On the other hand, there were some of my colleagues I thought I knew well or who had really impressed me. But once I was in the manager role, I could see that they were actually not doing as much as I thought they were. There were also policies and procedures I thought were ridiculous as a team member but as a manager I could see why they were in place . . . I was really surprised at how much my perspective changed within a matter of just a few weeks.

What should she have done instead?

Start out strong, for sure, but also with maturity and balance. You have to acknowledge the big change and assume command of the team; take charge; accept the mantle of authority. You do *not* need to explain why you were the right one for the promotion. You don't need to justify why you are now the boss. Instead, assume your position and explain how you are going to operate as the new manager. Ms. Finance told me, "I wish I had just said, 'I've been honored to be part of this team. Now I'm honored to be the manager of this team. We all have existing relationships. Those relationships will change to greater and lesser degrees now that I am your manager. I take this responsibility very seriously. I am committed to being really good at it. I am hoping you will help me.'"

That would be a very good start. Then it's time for the "Good news!" management message. And end that first team meeting by scheduling your first one-on-ones with every one of your new direct reports.

But don't forget that you don't know what you don't know. Ms. Finance did learn from her own early missteps and could reflect: "Yes, coming from within gave me a huge advantage as the manager, because I did know the operation very well and the people . . . But the big lesson for me was that I had huge blind spots. I absolutely needed to unlearn some of my assumptions and biases, unload some of my baggage, and relearn the operation from a new perspective. In retrospect, I wish I had basically taken the approach of almost pretending I was a new manager coming in from the outside and starting fresh."

MANAGEMENT CHALLENGE #2:
WHEN COMING FROM THE OUTSIDE TO TAKE OVER LEADERSHIP OF AN EXISTING TEAM

When you are the new manager taking over leadership of an existing team, you are coming into a whole scene with its own backstory. You are a new character: the outsider. Your new direct reports, on the other hand, are the insiders. They very likely have plenty of baggage with each other already. The question on everybody's mind right now is simple: Who the heck are you to be taking over their team?

As the new leader of an existing team, you are, in all likelihood, replacing a boss who has recently departed—by being either promoted or demoted—or is altogether gone now, voluntarily or otherwise. In any case, you are filling somebody else's shoes. Rest assured that some of your new employees will feel that absolutely nobody can fill the previous manager's shoes. Others will feel their lot can only improve under new leadership. Still others might have been internal candidates for the job and resentful that an outsider was brought in for the position instead.

As the outsider, you've got to figure out who's who on the team. Every employee comes to work with a different level of ability and skill. They come with different backgrounds, personalities, styles, ways of communicating, work habits, and motivations. Some of them need more guidance than others. They all already know each other, more or less. And it's not just your direct reports you'll have to figure out, but also your own boss and all the other managers at your level and above who have dealings with your new team. You have a lot of new relationships to build.

Meanwhile, you're going to be hot on the trail of figuring out what's what. If you are new to the entire organization, you've got an extra layer of orientation and learning to do. In any event, you need to learn the nuts and bolts of your new job and then start learning the nuts and bolts of the job of every one of your direct reports. If you are also a new employee, you need to be welcomed, introduced, onboarded, oriented, and brought up to speed.

While your new employer likely offers a new hire orientation program, it is often sparse and inadequate, especially to get up to speed in a leadership role.

Start looking for resources from which you can start teaching yourself:

- The organization's big picture: its vision, mission, values, and culture
- Where your team fits in the organization: the work of the team
- Broad performance standards, workplace expectations
- Company systems, practices, procedures

Some of this material may be covered in the formal orientation process. If so, get your hands on documentation. The more documentation you can study, the better. Ask whoever did the orientation program for more learning resources. Ask HR, your new colleagues, your boss. As you are studying these resources, take good notes and formulate good questions.

Meanwhile, in all likelihood you were not hired solely to be a manager. You will probably have plenty of new tasks, responsibilities, and projects in addition to managing. And this is a new job for you. So you have some very job-specific learning to do too. Get your hands on as many learning resources as you possibly can for self-study. Start with the current projects, tasks, and responsibilities being handled on the team. Which of these projects, tasks, and responsibilities will you specifically own? For each, find or ask for:

- Examples of past work product and work in progress
- Background materials, standard operating procedures, instructions, manuals, checklists, or other job aids, and answers to frequently asked questions
- Key people on and outside the team with whom you'll be working

You would learn all of this eventually in the course of doing the job, but if you want to accelerate your up-so-speed learning, get your hands on these resources as quickly as you can.

Meanwhile, as early on as you can, try to identify individuals who might be able to help you accelerate your learning—internal experts, other managers, colleagues, and of course your boss—who can provide a human voice to help you understand all you are researching. Whether or not anybody has gone to the trouble to fill your schedule in your first several weeks with one-on-one sessions, you should pursue scheduled one-on-ones with every key player you can identify. Go to every one-on-one with a clear learning agenda. Start with this open-ended question: "If you were in my shoes right now, what are the things you would want to know?" Your best line in these conversations is going to be something like: "Will you please tell me more about that?" Take lots of notes.

The most important factor in your onboarding and up-to-speed process is not 100 percent in your control. You need to work hard to get as much structured one-on-one time with your (maybe new) boss as you possibly can. Try to get time every day. At first, concentrate on what you are learning of the big picture, the work of your team, the broad performance standards, and companywide processes. Discuss your notes and ask your questions. Over time, your one-on-ones with your boss will move on to your specific tasks, responsibilities, and projects.

Of course, your first and foremost responsibility will be managing your new direct reports. From the outset, make perfectly clear to your manager how you intend to manage your direct reports. Explain that you are committed to being a strong, highly engaged manager. Explain that you plan to follow the best practices of the regular, ongoing, structured one-on-one dialogue. Make clear that you intend to be rigorous about spelling out expectations, tracking performance, holding people accountable, and helping employees earn what they need through their performance. In the early stages of your new role, you might even encourage your boss to sit in on some of your one-on-one meetings in order to give your boss clear insight into how you are managing.

Everyone on your team is still going to be wondering: "Who are you?" "What are your plans?" "How will you manage?" And "What will it all mean for me?" You are the new boss, after all. You'll have to have a team meeting. You'll have to make a speech, the "Good news!" speech, as outlined in New Manager Challenge #1. Your new employees are bound to have lots of questions. You might have to devote a whole Q&A session to how your management style is going to work. It's a very good idea to end that first team meeting by scheduling your first one-on-one with each direct report.

Your new employees are likely to have as many answers as they have questions—strong opinions about what should change and what should stay the same. Because you are the outsider, new to everyone, it's important to have a series of team meetings in the early stages of your new regime. You need a forum where you can say the same things to everybody in the same way at the same time, in which everybody can speak on the record in front of each other, hear each other, and respond spontaneously. You need the light of public disclosure and discussion, at least for a little while. Depending on the group dynamics, more or less information may come out in a team meeting format. My advice to new managers in this situation is to stage a series of brainstorming sessions around three questions:

1. What should change about how our team operates?
2. What should not change?
3. If you were suddenly the team manager, what would be your first, second, and third priorities?

The ground rules are simple: Everybody is required to participate. Comments must be about work performance only, not about personal traits and characteristics of any individual. I recommend sitting in a circle if the group is not too big. That way you can go around the circle (clockwise or counterclockwise) for each question, getting everyone to respond to the first; then everyone responds to the second, and then to the third. Depending on the size of the group and the amount of baggage people are carrying, this can take hours. You might want to split it into three separate sessions.

As a new manager, you will be amazed at how much you learn from this process. You will gather key data from your new team about what they think is working and what they think is not working. At the same time, you'll learn a great deal about each of them and their working relationships from their responses to these questions. Take notes in these sessions, taking special note of any point from one of your new employees that you'd like to follow up on in a one-on-one discussion. These follow-up discussions will reinforce to your new direct reports that you are listening and taking their input seriously. As well, you will make it clear that you are paying attention to details and documenting every step of the way.

Beware, however, of letting these "brainstorming" sessions take on their own life and go on unabated. After you've taken in everybody's input, in short order, you want to make sure you never lose the spirit or habit of constantly learning from everybody's input. But once the discussions start going round and round over the same ground, that's your cue to make some decisions and pivot the group discussion to make it very clear: "Here's what's staying the same. Here's what's changing. The following will be our top three priorities for the foreseeable future." About the same time you are ready to make that pivot, that's also a pretty good time to shift the balance of workplace communication sharply *away* from the team-meeting format and start concentrating on your one-on-ones.

As you start your substantive one-on-ones in earnest, your first mission with every direct report will be to get up to speed on the fundamentals of his job. Ask him about his current projects, task, and responsibilities. For each:

- Review examples of past work product and current work in progress.
- Review background materials, standard operating procedures, instructions, manuals, checklists, or other job aids, as well as answers to frequently asked questions.
- Talk to key people inside and outside the team with whom the employee works regularly.
- Look for opportunities to shadow the employee and watch him do the work.

In the first few weeks you should meet often with every person. With this systematic approach, you will get up to speed in a matter of weeks and be in a position to provide at least some guidance and support. Over time, your conversations will become more knowledgeable and your ability to give direction increasingly acute. You will be amazed at how quickly you can get yourself up to full operating capacity as a manager in this way.

WHEN BRINGING TOGETHER AN ENTIRELY NEW TEAM

This is a special twist on the "new manager" situation, when everybody is new to you *and* to each other. You have not met each other yet. You are not sure how long this team will even exist. You didn't get to choose the team. As far as you know, nobody on the team has ever worked together before. You do know that you have, let's say, eight people, at least to start. Some more experienced than others, of course.

None of this is out of the ordinary. It's a start-up situation of one kind or another. Start-up company, department, workgroup, project team. We see this in professional services, especially consulting, IT implementations, Hollywood (or elsewhere) movies, political campaigns, and so on.

Here's the challenge: Your team has a bunch of work to get done, very well, very fast, all day long, in pursuit of a mission, right now and for the duration of the project. It's just that none of the team members have ever worked together. Beyond the team, there are many other internal customers and vendors you'll all have to deal with, all very likely equally new to everybody. Maybe you have some standard operating procedures to guide you, but for the most part your new team has not yet established any habits or norms of interaction. Most everything is starting from scratch.

You are as new to the situation as the rest of the team and will have to create a rigorous orientation program for yourself, as any new manager of team would coming in from the outside. (See Challenge #2, earlier.) But in this case, you have the added challenge that everybody is new to the work and to each other.

What do you do? Where do you start?

With a brand new team you have no baggage. Nothing is broken. You have the chance to start things off right from the outset.

Here's the first pitfall to avoid. "Everyone hit the ground running!" It sounds great, at first. Self-starting high-performers want to dive in. The problem is that when everyone hits the ground running without good coordination, people often go running off in their own directions. Before long, people find they are tripping over each other, duplicating work in one area while leaving gaps in another, or unwittingly taking noncomplementary approaches to the shared work. On day one, you need to make sure every individual knows exactly where he or she fits in the team and where the team fits in the larger picture. You need to get everybody on the same page, everybody on the same plan, and everybody ready to march together in the same direction.

Managers in this situation ask me all the time, "Is there any way to accelerate the relationship-building and create connections quickly?"

Many to try to find a shortcut by focusing on the personal, whether that's going out for drinks or dinner, shopping together at lunchtime, playing golf or tennis, or running together over the weekend. Maybe team members find they have in common their taste in movies, fitness, family. Or they both have kids (or not), come from the same town, or have been to the same destination.

But it turns out that when new team members spend their initial bonding time focusing on what they have in common outside of work, they often fail to explore how they will or will not fit together *at work*. Those things we have in common outside of work often tell us strikingly little about how well we are likely to work together. Indeed, sometimes building connections around "off duty" interests can make it harder to confront issues at work.

Another strategy is helping people connect with each other through team-building exercises. Maybe the team builds a house together on day one to get to know each other. Or runs a relay race together. Or practices "trust falls," where you fall backward into each other's arms. There is a place for this sort of off-site team-building activity, but it is often more of a distraction than anything else. Why take the long way around? At the outset, you need to get everybody focused on the shared *work*. Everybody needs to get to know each other in terms of who each person is *at work*.

On day one, as part of the first team meeting, after you've introduced yourself and the process by which you intend to lead the team, facilitate an introduction process that focuses on "Who I Am at Work":

- Everyone needs to introduce him/herself: "This is who I am at work. This is my portfolio of experiences. This is what I can do. This is how I operate, and these are my work habits. This is the commitment I am willing to make to this team." As the leader, you start. Introduce yourself first. Then give everyone a chance to introduce him/herself to the group.

- Introductions work a whole lot better if people have a chance to prepare in advance. So before you have everyone chime in at the table, stop and give each person a chance to conduct a brief self-assessment.

- Some organizations use elaborate self-assessment tools, and many individuals will have a sense of their own "profiles" if they've gone through that process. That suggests a good first question: "Have you ever participated in a self-profiling assessment? If so, what did you learn about yourself from that assessment that will help others work better with you?"

- What do people on the team need to know about how you work that will help them work better with you? Here I must offer any self-assessing person the following caution: Be authentic. Don't pretend to be something you are not. But also present your best self. Don't let yourself off the hook. Hold yourself to a high standard. This is the perfect opportunity to say, "I struggle to remain organized, so please hold me to a high standard. Please tell me if I am undermining myself. Give me pointers if you have them. I will do my best." This is *not* the opportunity to say, "I'm just not organized, so don't expect me to be."

- The best practice for the introduction session is to first have everybody conduct their own brief self-assessment. Then, if you have time, it's very productive to have people pair off in twos (with one trio if you have an uneven number) and interview each other based on the self-assessments. Third, have each pair collaborate on introducing each other to the rest of the group.

For any new-new team, the first expedition should be intelligence gathering. The best way to end that first team meeting is with a whole list of unanswered questions. Make it a good list by brainstorming with everybody at the table: What don't we know that we need to know in order to make a smarter plan for our work as a team? Some of those questions will naturally go to you as the team leader. The rest of the questions should be divided among the team members. Sharing preliminary answers to these questions should be the opening gambit of the second team meeting, within a matter of hours or days. Of course, some questions will be unanswerable. Some will be overtaken by events. Still, the second team meeting should be focused on: What have we been able to learn?

Defining Roles and Responsibilities

Early on, you need to clarify individual roles and responsibilities for every single member of the team. Often you will be given individuals who are presumptively slotted for a specific position. Maybe you are given a third baseman, a shortstop, a left-fielder, but what you really need is a pitcher. In any event, you rarely get to choose all of the individuals who will make up your team—or any of them, for that matter. Even if you get to choose them, you may not be able to find the ideal candidates. Your team will be made up of the players you have.

Your job as the leader is to figure out how to make the best use of each player and leverage all of the players on the team, together, in concert with each other. That means you should try to do your best due diligence on each team member before you assign roles and responsibilities. How much information can you get on each member of the team in advance? Resumes, letters of recommendation, prior project reviews, regular reviews, prior work product? Ideally, you should review a robust paper trail for each member of the team in advance of managing them. That's not always available. In the absence of that kind of information, you might consider an interview-style one-on-one with every member of the team in between the first and second team meetings. You need to know who you are dealing with and exactly what human capital assets you have to work with on this team.

By the third team meeting, you need to create a clear delineation of roles and responsibilities. Make it 100 percent clear what role each person is going to play. Who owns which tasks, responsibilities, and projects or project components? Who is expected to do what, exactly, and how, where, and when?

Of course, you'll be meeting with every person one-on-one on a regular basis, spelling out expectations, following up, providing feedback, troubleshooting, keeping score, and correcting course when necessary. And you'll meet together as a team whenever there are conversations in which everybody needs to participate.

MANAGEMENT CHALLENGE #4:
WHEN YOU ARE WELCOMING A NEW
MEMBER TO YOUR EXISTING TEAM

Managers often realize that welcoming a new member will be a big change for the members of the team, usually for some more than others. And of course, it is a career move–sized change for the new team member. However, it is not always so obvious just how significant a change this may be for you, the manager.

One new team member can really shift the dynamic of a team. The prospect of a new person (let's call her "Newby") joining the team will set off a cascade of powerful reactions. Less so perhaps than the prospect of a new manager. But still plenty. Your direct reports will wonder: "Will Newby be a long-termer or just passing through?" "Will she be a star or a loser?" "Will she be a loner or find a best friend?" "Will she be on my side? Or someone else's?" "What will it all mean for me?"

For you as the manager, with any luck some of these questions should already be answered, at least preliminarily. After all, you chose to hire Newby. So you are probably already a big fan. Beware of falling into the classic hiring manager's error: don't fool yourself into thinking that the person you interviewed is going to line up exactly with the person who shows up at work and becomes part of your team. No matter how rigorous your hiring process may be, Newby was doing her absolute best to put her best foot forward every step of the way. She was telling you everything you wanted to hear with her most persuasive delivery. (Can you blame her?) Not only that, but the more you started to like Newby in the hiring process, the more you may have put your hopes and dreams for this position onto Newby. You might well have started to see a lot of what you really *wanted* to see in Newby and overlooked any signs to the contrary. I've seen this happen so many times. It is only natural that you have a honeymoon period. Just don't be heartbroken when Newby turns out to be human. Don't blame Newby when she turns out to *not* be the completely Self-Managing-Superhero-Answer-to-All-of-Your-Problems (nobody is).

No matter how great Newby may be, I promise you, she will need to be managed, more closely at first than you would probably guess, and for longer. Be prepared to spend a lot of time at the outset working closely with Newby. You can't wait for her to ask. She might not realize how much onboarding support and up-to-speed coaching she needs. Even if she does realize, she likely won't ask for it.

While some employers are better at this than others, most employers have only a minimal process for welcoming new employees and getting them on board and up to speed. There's usually even less support for an individual who is a current employee transferring internally to another department or team. At best, even in organizations with robust orientation and training programs, there is the inevitable hand-off to the hiring manager when the formal process is complete. That's exactly where the ball is so often dropped. Newby could be forgiven for assuming that your organization has a good process. *You*, on the other hand, cannot be forgiven for assuming that. Making sure that Newby gets on board and up to speed properly is your responsibility. It's certainly going to be your problem if it doesn't go well.

Unless you happen to work for the United States Armed Forces and your organization's orientation program looks a lot like boot camp, you should not count on the formal process. From the first day Newby joins your team, you need to take 100 percent responsibility for making sure she is welcomed properly and given the onboarding support and up-to-speed coaching she will need to become a fully functioning member of the team.

That does not mean delegating the responsibility to one of your lieutenants. So often managers tell me, "Oh yeah, I pay very close attention to getting new people on board and up to speed. My lieutenant handles all of that for me."

Clue: if someone—anyone—"handles all that" for you, then you are not paying close enough attention to it. The onboarding of any new employee who will report directly to you should be handled by you. You can start by explaining that your modus operandi for managing is to build a regular, ongoing, structured one-on-one dialogue with every person who reports to you. So you will start by scheduling a lot of one-on-ones at the outset: maybe two per day initially, once at the beginning of the workday and again at the end of the day.

What will you talk about in your one-on-ones during the onboarding process? You need to be prepared with a list of initial learning objectives:

- The organization, big picture: Its vision, mission, values, and culture
- Where your team fits in the organization: The work of the team
- Broad performance standards, workplace expectations
- Company systems, practices, procedures

Some of this material may have been covered in the formal orientation process, but it is all well worth repeating in detail repeatedly. You need to have these conversations with your new employees yourself so that you can add your voice and your interpretation and your points of emphasis. After all, Newby is going to be answering to *you*.

Once you've hammered away at these fundamentals, shift your one-on-ones to helping the new employee really dig in and start to understand the context of the work she will be doing. That's why the next set of learning objectives should be very job specific. First discuss the current projects, tasks, and responsibilities being handled on the team. Then explain which projects, tasks, and responsibilities Newby will be working on. For each, offer:

- Examples of past work product, and work in progress
- Background materials, standard operating procedures, instructions, manuals, checklists, or other job aids, as well as answers to frequently asked questions
- Key people on and outside of the team with whom the new employee will work
- Opportunities to practice, rehearse, shadow, dry-run, scrimmage, rough-draft, or what-have-you, as appropriate
- Key players on and outside of the team

Though this is the kind of information that the new employee would gather eventually on the job, it is much more effective to learn it systematically according to a clear agenda, with learning resources provided along the way.

Take special note: if Newby is going to be responsible for managing others, then in your one-on-ones with her you need to make it clear immediately that you expect her to manage her direct reports in a strong, highly engaged manner. Explain what that means in detail:

You expect Newby to manage her direct reports by following the same management best practices that you follow, with regular, ongoing, structured one-on-one dialogue.

You expect Newby in her one-on-one with her direct reports to spell out expectations clearly, track performance closely, and help employees earn what they need through their performance.

Newby's management responsibilities should be her number-one priority, and that means they should be among your top priorities too, until you are certain that Newby is both up to speed in her own operational knowledge and consistently engaging her direct reports in regular one-on-ones. Thereafter, you will need to manage how Newby manages, just as you do with any other manager who reports to you. In the early stages of teaching your new manager to be highly engaged, you may want to sit in on some of your managers' one-on-one meetings with their employees to gain more insight for coaching the new manager on managing.

With a concrete onboarding plan, clear learning objectives, and supporting materials—and one or two daily one-on-ones—you will be amazed at how quickly you can get a new employee on board, up to speed, and operating at full capacity. In the process, you will also introduce that new employee to the wonders of high-structure, high-substance dialogue. Even if you meet just once a day for the first three weeks, the new employee will get into the habit.

With lots of learning materials to go along with the objectives you've laid out in the onboarding plan, of course, the new employee has plenty of self-study work she could do in between meetings with you. Plus Newby will pick up opportunities here and there to sit in on meetings and perhaps to shadow employees doing related work.

Generally, in the first several weeks of employment there is a lot of running around, but much of the time is often relatively unstructured. Usually much of that unstructured time ends up alongside one or two or three of Newby's new colleagues, ultimately following a schedule that is somewhat inadvertent. Newby might formally or informally buddy up with those colleagues and start taking cues from them. I've seen it over and over again. The manager is working double-time to get Newby up to speed, but thirty hours a week, Newby is also getting a lot of input from her colleagues. Keep your eye on that. Make sure that Newby is not taking her cues from the wrong colleagues.

The solution is to make sure the new employee's schedule is highly structured for the first several weeks, not just in one-on-ones with you, but also in regular one-on-ones with everybody else. Don't leave the use of that valuable time to chance. Yes, you need to make sure to leave some time each day for the new employee's self-study of learning resources you provide. But fill up most of Newby's schedule in the first few days with one-on-ones with all those key players inside and outside the team. And provide a learning agenda for Newby to follow in those one-on-ones. After a few weeks of one-on-ones with everybody, Newby will have established ongoing dialogues with every individual with whom she will be working. At first, each dialogue will help Newby get up to speed. Over time, the dialogues will transform, and what they'll be discussing is the actual work they are now doing together.

CHAPTER THREE

The Challenges of Teaching Self-Management

How many of your employees always come to work a little early, stay a little late, make very good use of their time, use good systems to stay organized, make good decisions, and generally gets things done? Most managers I talk to have very few employees who are such masters of self-management. More likely, they have direct reports who sometimes come in a little late or leave a little early, take too many breaks, miss deadlines, waste other people's time, lose track of information, and/or become stymied by decision making.

The more an employee struggles with the fundamentals of self-management, the less work that person is going get done and the more errors he is going to make. Of that much, I probably don't need to convince you. So why do so many managers struggle with managing the self-management fundamentals of their employees?

Ask yourself:

- When do you talk with your direct reports about being on time? When do you mention not leaving early? Or taking too many breaks?

- When do you talk with direct reports about not preparing enough for a meeting? Or sending poorly thought out emails? Or otherwise wasting other people's time?

- When do you discuss losing track of information?
- When do you review bad decisions?

Usually, when managers talk with their direct reports about matters of self-management, it is a conversation about failure—often petty failure, sometimes an accumulation of petty failures. If you don't know how to have that conversation, it can feel rather awkward, especially with a fellow adult. That's because we take for granted that adults should be able to (and expected to) manage themselves without being told.

Managers often say to me, "Do I really have to tell my employees to be on time, stay all day, and not take too many long breaks? I don't want them to think I'm treating them like children." Yet they have employees who sometimes come in late, leave early, and take long breaks, not to mention those who sometimes waste time (their own and others'). Too often managers let the problems slide until there is a big one or just too many. By then it may be a big deal: the employee has a demonstrated track record of failure on some basic element of self-management.

It's tempting to just write off an employee who fails repeatedly on some basic element of self-management. Such failures can make employees appear deficient in their natural ability or basic competency. They might seem lazy, flaky, clueless, disorganized, stupid, or some combination of the above. Those would be character flaws that simply can't be fixed by any manager. But often this conclusion is very far from the truth. Many employees fail because somehow they never learned the fundamentals of time management, organization, and problem solving. When you teach those employees, they tend to get a whole lot better, and often they are very grateful.

When I say this to managers, sometimes they reply, "I'm sorry, but it's just not my job to teach my employees how to manage themselves. They are adults. They should already know how to manage themselves when they walk in the door on day one. If they don't, it is their responsibility to figure it out, to learn it on the job." But managers cannot possibly hire employees who are all already 100 percent masters of self-management. Employees who are not already masters of self-management will need guidance, direction, and support to build up their self-management skills on the job. And it really matters.

So you have no choice. It is your job to make sure your direct reports learn and practice the fundamentals of self-management. You first need to decide which fundamentals really matter in your workplace. Then you need to make those fundamentals of self-management performance requirements for everybody. Trumpet them loud and clear. Then talk about those fundamentals in your one-on-ones—as needed, of course. Recognize and reward those who are masters of self-management. Learn from them: in their best practices and special tricks, there may be lessons for those who struggle with the fundamentals. As for those who really struggle, you have a chance to build them up and make them better by giving them some of the basic tools and techniques of timeliness, organization, and problem solving.

Teaching Good Self-Management
Is a Leadership Coup

It's pretty hard to find good examples of organizations that systematically teach self-management and build highly self-managing players as a key component of their workplace culture. One example does comes to mind: the military. Over the years, I've had the tremendous honor of doing work for various branches of the United States Armed Forces. People associate the highly regimented lifestyle of the military with its strict chain of command and rules. Soldiers follow orders. How is that a good example of teaching self-management?

The United States Armed Forces are famously effective at teaching leadership. What is less obvious to some is the other side of that equation: followership. Before anybody learns to lead, first they learn to follow—follow the highly regimented schedule, procedures, rules, orders, chain of command. The fact that everybody in the military learns to follow makes it a whole lot easier for leaders to lead. It also makes it easier for soldiers to know what to do, when, where, and how.

Here's something else that's not so obvious: Self-management does not mean, "Do whatever you want whenever, wherever, and however you want." There's no management whatsoever involved in that scenario. Even if it were 100 percent up to the individual what to do, when, where, and how, she would need to make a schedule and procedures to follow in order to get anything done. When an employee has a clear schedule and procedures, it's a whole lot easier.

Granted, the military takes an extremely comprehensive approach to the teaching of self-management. I'm not suggesting that you tell your employees what time to wake up and what time to go to sleep, or address people by rank and salute. In most workplaces, that would be a little bit much.

Focus on the fundamentals. Our research shows that there are four fundamentals of self-management that virtually all managers agree they'd like to see in their direct reports:

1. Time management
2. Interpersonal communication
3. Organizational skills
4. Basic problem solving

How do you teach employees these fundamentals in the midst of all the work everybody needs to get done? Start with very clear performance standards. Then coach every single person on them in your regular ongoing one-on-ones, as needed.

Coaching on time management does not necessarily mean that you tell employees exactly what time to come to work, what time to take breaks, and what time to leave. Time management means planning and working to optimize your time and always being sure to make only good use of others' time. Here's a great bonus: it turns out that when employees get really good at time management, they usually gain more control over their own schedules. Scheduling flexibility is one of the things employees want and value the most.

Coaching on interpersonal communication does not mean you tell employees exactly what to say and what not to say, every step of the way. You might need to teach some of the old-fashioned fundamentals, like good manners. You might need to teach people to err on the side of in-person communication rather than electronic communication, and to look people in the eye when speaking in person. If you're doing regular one-on-ones for several weeks, then the structure of your ongoing dialogue itself should help retrain the employee in more professional communication habits.

Coaching on organizational skills does not mean that you tell employees exactly how, where, and when to handle every single task, responsibility, and project. Organization means using good systems to keep track of guidelines, specifications, expectations, timelines, and measurable concrete actions every step of the way. Another great bonus: it turns out that when employees get really good at using systems to stay organized, they usually gain more discretion in how they do their work.

Coaching on problem solving does not mean you need to anticipate every single problem an individual could possibly face and give her standing orders for every scenario. But you should have standing orders for regularly occurring problems. One more bonus: when employees are well trained in implementing established solutions to recurring problems, they usually get better and better at extrapolating from those solutions to improvise in the face of unanticipated problems.

You can teach self-management, and it works. All you need to do is build it into your regular, ongoing, strong, highly engaged leadership. Focus on the fundamentals. Just like every other aspect of performance, build it into your team communications and talk about it on a regular basis in your one-on-one dialogues. Teach it. Require it. Measure it. Reward people when they do it. Hold people to account when they don't.

Most employees will benefit tremendously from your investment in teaching them the fundamentals and be very grateful for it. Of course, they won't always be lucky enough to have you for a manager. If you've succeeded in teaching just one employee the fundamentals of self-management, you will have given him skills that will make him more valuable anywhere he goes, no matter what he does—skills that will never become obsolete.

MANAGEMENT CHALLENGE #5:
WHEN EMPLOYEES HAVE A HARD TIME MANAGING TIME

Time is precious. Everybody gets just 168 hours in a week. Employees almost always want more free time and more control over their own schedules. Managers typically see employees' time as a business resource to be optimized. Thus an incessant tug-of-war over time is always being played out.

Before you engage in any tug-of-war over time management with any of your employees, first make sure you really understand the true time requirements of the jobs in question. In certain jobs it is critical that employees be faithful to a very precise schedule; those are jobs for which the employee's physical presence at a specific place and time is essential to his/her work. It could be a factory where shifts are timed to keep the production machinery working around the clock. In retail, somebody needs to be there to open the store, first thing, and close the store, last thing, not to mention in between when customers want to shop. In a hospital, you need coverage all the time because you can't have patients there without health care providers. Whenever coverage is the critical time management factor, everybody has much less flexibility, so everybody needs to work harder to make it work.

There are other jobs in which the key is to be available at a moment's notice, such as doctors, police officers, and firefighters.

On-call work is the extreme on both sides of flexibility. Whenever one is on call, the employee's time is not really free. Yet on-call arrangements allow employers to be leaner in their staffing while maintaining coverage, and at the same time they give some employees more time at least "almost off."

Still many other types of work have the potential to be much more flexible. Lots of work can be done by mutual appointment; for example, real estate sales or financial advising. There is increasingly more work that can be done really any time, as long as it's done by a certain deadline; for example web design or data analysis. Even work that requires considerable interdependency can be done on a flexible schedule as long as those who are working together remain in regular high-quality communication.

I find it baffling when a manager struggles with an employee about being faithful to a very specific schedule when the work of that employee really doesn't need to be done in a particular place at a particular time. Why engage in that tug-of-war if it's not necessary? Employees really value flexibility, and you can sometimes offer it as a very powerful reward in exchange for high performance. If the job can be done within a flexible schedule, there is no sense in fighting unnecessary battles about adherence to a specific schedule.

Trumpet the value of time—everybody's time. Remind people frequently and enthusiastically how valuable everybody's time truly is, and insist that everybody's time be respected.

What about the employee who is chronically late, leaves early, or takes too many breaks? What is to be done with employees who simply cannot live by a simple schedule? Tardiness, leaving early, and taking too many breaks: These issues seem so petty as performance problems go. Why do these problems nag away at managers?

In some cases, managers are right to attribute these problems to an employee's blasé attitude or a lack of care, consideration, or diligence. When that's the source of the problem, there is no substitute for constant reminders in your regular one-on-ones. Just by focusing on it, you are likely to make it better, at least for a little while:

> *You:* "You're late."
>
> *Employee:* "I know. I'm sorry. I overslept."
>
> *You:* "You are supposed to be on time."
>
> *Employee:* "I know. I'm sorry. There was bad traffic."
>
> *You:* "You need to be on time."
>
> *Employee:* "Yes. I'll try to do better."

The employee is probably going to be on time the next day. Maybe he will be on time for a while. Until the next time he's late. Do you have the same conversation again? How many times? You have to be the judge of when too much is too much. When somebody does actually get fired for coming in late (or leaving early, or taking too many breaks), everybody else usually gets the message. At least for a while.

Believe it or not, you'll find that some people have never really mastered the fundamentals of living by a schedule. You may be the first person to hold them accountable for being on time. In the process, you might end up doing this person a huge favor.

I've heard countless stories like this one from a very experienced call center manager:

> I had one employee who was always on time for the evening shift but always late for the early morning shift. Sometimes it makes sense to just put someone like that on the late shift where he is on time. Of course, I didn't want to reward him for being late in the morning, but I also didn't want to keep setting him up for failure by having him do the early morning shift, because he was obviously having a hard time with that. Funny enough, when I talked with him about it, it turned out that he preferred the early morning shift! The early morning shift was the tougher one to staff, so it's good to have people who want to work the early morning. I just had to figure out a way to manage him to success.

This guy was young and inexperienced, and he confessed that
he really needed some help. I had to help him learn how to
be on time. So I taught him how to make and use a schedule.
At first, I wrote out a schedule for him, working backward from
the 5:00 A.M. start time: "Walk in the front door here at work at
4:55 A.M. That means driving away from home by 4:30 A.M. That
means you need to be out of bed by 3:45 A.M. What time do you
need to get to sleep the night before?"

The manager went on: "We made that little schedule, and then I
used that schedule to really talk him through it. I think it helped him
to just have it spelled out."

Sometimes managers ask me, "Is it appropriate to help an employee
plan out details for their after-work schedule? Or details as personal
as what time he goes to sleep and what time he gets out of bed?" My
answer: Only if the employee can't figure that stuff out on his own, sufficient to get to work on time and not leave early.

Are some employees insulted or annoyed by the explicit focus on
the petty details of living by a schedule? Perhaps they are. But almost
always they start coming in on time, staying all day, and taking fewer
breaks, at least for a while. Many employees will be genuinely grateful
for your helping them get better at living by a schedule.

What About Employees Who Sneak Out Early?

Sometimes they are just helping themselves to a little free time. Others
may have obligations after work that leave them pressed for time.
You may have to talk them through their after-work schedule so they
make sure they push back any obligations to a time that does not
require them to leave work early. Talk through what it is going to take
for that person to stay all the way until the end of his scheduled work
obligations. Spell it out. Break it down. Follow up. One technique I've
seen managers use is to schedule some very concrete to-do items for the
employee during the last hour of his work time in order to help him
stay focused up to the last minute.

What About Employees Who Take Too Many Breaks and Waste Time at Work?

The answer is the same. Talk about it, in no uncertain terms. Spell out what's required: at work you are expected to be focused on getting work done very well, very efficiently, all day long. Everyone has time wasters, but nobody can afford them. Help people identify their big time wasters and eliminate them altogether.

Most employees have more to do at work than they can fit into their work schedules and more they want to do outside work than they can do in their limited free time. Many are chronically overtired and seriously overscheduled. If they are chronically late, leave early, and take too many breaks, there is a good chance they would benefit greatly from some aggressive coaching on time management.

Setting priorities is usually step one in most time-management programs and seminars. If you have limited time and too much to do, then you need to set priorities—an order of precedence or preference—so that you control what gets done first, second, third, and so on. It is obvious to most professionals that setting priorities is the key to time management. The hard part is teaching employees how to set their priorities.

When it comes to the big picture, help them set clear priorities; then communicate with them relentlessly about those priorities. Make sure your direct reports are devoting the lion's share of their time to first and second priorities. When it comes to setting day-to-day priorities, teach them how by setting priorities together. Walk through it with them to share your thinking process: "This is first priority because X. This is second priority because Y. This is low priority because Z." Over time, you hope they learn. Until they learn, you have to keep making decisions with them or for them. Teach them to postpone low-priority activities until high-priority activities are well ahead of schedule. That opens the time windows during which lower-priority activities can be accomplished—starting with the top lower priorities, of course. Time wasters, on the other hand, should be eliminated altogether whenever possible.

One of the best gifts you can give anybody is teaching them how to maintain an old-fashioned time log to begin to understand how they actually use their time inside and outside of work. That way, they can start planning their time more effectively and eliminate time wasters. The tool is simple enough; the idea is that an individual keeps track of what she is doing, almost minute by minute. Each time the person changes from one activity to another, she notes briefly the time and the activity:

6:15 A.M.   Woke up; personal care

6:47 A.M.   Dressed, having breakfast

7:14 A.M.   In car leaving home

7:49 A.M.   Sat down at my desk, read through to-do list, set priorities for the day

8:10 A.M.   Got up to use bathroom and get coffee

8:28 A.M.   Sat back down at desk, opened email

8:29 A.M.   Started preparing response to email from manager

8:40 A.M.   Incoming phone call from Jones

9:15 A.M.   Continued preparing response to email

9:25 A.M.   Got up to chat with Smith

And so on. Used properly, a time log can be a powerful reality check and source of insight into how to help someone get much better at managing his time. Anyone can benefit from a time log, but anyone who is struggling to stay on time will almost surely benefit. Ask that person to use a time log and bring it to your regular one-on-ones. Use the data from the time log to coach the person to look for opportunities to eliminate time wasters, put priorities in order, make a realistic schedule, and live by it.

What About Employees Who Miss Deadlines?

Managing an employee who works on deadlines is a bit different from managing those who work on specific schedules. When an employee is working on a specific goal that must be delivered at a very specific time, typically the manager has much more room to give the employee more control over his schedule along the way. An employee working under deadline pressure might end up working more than if he were on a regular schedule. But he probably has more flexibility as to when to do the work.

Sometimes that flexibility is hard for people to manage. Without the structure of a specific schedule, some people have a hard time remaining productive and efficient. That's why anybody without a set schedule needs a good plan.

If you eliminate time-wasting and account for unexpected diversions, 99 percent of missed deadlines are missed because their plan was no good in the first place. Any employee who misses deadlines needs to get much better at planning. Although you can send that person to a class in basic project planning, you need to dedicate some of your one-on-one time—at least for some period of time—to teaching this person how to make a plan and how to work a plan. Start teaching the fundamentals of planning by working with the employee in your regular one-on-ones to rigorously plan his work.

You don't have to do all the work of planning for this employee. In fact, you really shouldn't. Make the employee's next assignment to make his own comprehensive plan for his primary responsibilities and projects. Use your one-on-one time to work on the plan together, providing guidance and feedback along the way. Take that person's current bigger goals, one by one; separate them into intermediate benchmarks along the way; and break the intermediate benchmarks into smaller goals and deadlines along the way. Then look at those smaller goals and deadlines and map out the concrete actions necessary to reach each of them, including a timetable for the concrete actions. That's how you lay out the work, piece by piece, into a realistic plan of action.

Delegation 101 is really synonymous with teaching employees the fundamentals of planning. Delegation 101 is all about clearly articulating goals, specifications, and deadlines. I've long used this example: "I want you to create a box by Tuesday at 3:00 P.M. It must be a wooden box, smaller than a refrigerator and bigger than a breadbox. It cannot be yellow, though gold is an option. (Do you understand the difference between yellow and gold?) Those are the specifications." If you want to help this person make a plan for making the box, here's where you go next: "To be done by Tuesday at 3 P.M., let's figure out all of the specific concrete actions that must be taken along the way. What are all the smaller goals that need to be done in order to complete this box? Now, to be done by Tuesday at 3 P.M., what needs to be completed by Tuesday at noon? What about Tuesday at 9 A.M.? So where do we need to be by Monday at the end of the day? What does that mean about the weekend? Do we need to plan to work the weekend, or can we get where we need to be by Friday, end of day?"

In your ongoing one-on-ones, you figure out, over time, with each employee:

- How big should the goals be?
- How far out should the deadlines be?
- How many guidelines are necessary with each goal?
- What are the intermediate and smaller goals along the way, and what is the timeline for those? These are always moving targets. That's why there is no end in sight to this discussion. It's just another part of your ongoing one-on-one dialogue.

When you are working with an employee who has struggled to meet deadlines, there is a simple rule: Start small. Teach that employee to deliver on one very small goal with a very short deadline and meets all the specifications. Then maybe a little bit bigger. And then a little bigger still. Over time you can move toward projects with more ambitious goals and longer deadlines. As an employee demonstrates proficiency and performance, gradually increase the amount and importance of the work you assign, until you reach that person's appropriate scope of responsibility. Once that employee reaches that point, you can continue to empower her by using project planning tools together. Help her develop long-term project plans, complete with clear benchmarks along the way. Focus your one-on-one meetings on evaluating her progress toward each benchmark. Provide feedback and recommend adjustments every step of the way. Over time, she will be able to handle even bigger, more complex projects. If you make rigorous use of project planning tools as a centerpiece of your one-on-ones with this person, she is very likely to get continuously better at making and working a plan.

Then follow up in your regular one-on-ones, guiding, directing, and supporting every step of the way, revising the plan based on real-time data. Working a plan requires paying very close attention to external factors as well as internal progress. That means tracking the short-term goals very closely, continually accounting for how long each step is actually taking, and revising and adjusting along the way as needed.

Planning is not something you do in advance, set in stone, and then follow. For one thing, often what looks like a perfectly good plan on paper turns out to be a bit of a fantasy—a wishful projection. Every day I hear stories about meticulously crafted plans, very carefully broken out into short-term goals with short-term deadlines along the way, that nonetheless reflect completely unrealistic time lines. Sometimes they are just guesses—some more educated than others. In the real world, plans are always a work in progress. They need to be continually revised and adjusted, and that discussion should occur in your ongoing one-on-one dialogues.

Sometimes, in monitoring progress, it becomes clear that the employee simply must pick up the pace in order to meet the deadline. For example, "You are getting a hundred units done per day. At a hundred units per day times five days a week, you will only have a thousand units at the end of two weeks. That means you need to either work faster or work more hours."

If the plan is a good one and the goals are realistic, but short-term goals are still being missed, you need to go down onto the scene and watch closely to see what's going wrong. Is there an obstacle slowing down performance that you can remove? Is there a resource missing that you can provide? Is there a shortcut that the employee does not use? Are there diversions? Time-wasters? Sometimes there's just not enough fire in the belly. When reasonable short-term goals are being missed, sometimes all you can do is drill down and coach: "If you have one hundred phone calls to make, you start with the first one, move on to the second, and then the third, and so on. Each call is a concrete action. Every concrete action can be broken down into smaller components, and each small component is, itself, another concrete action. If you get bogged down with the feeling that you are "not getting anything done," break every task into its smaller components and start tackling them one at a time. You will start moving forward.

With some employees, that kind of intensive, granular, step-by-step coaching can make the difference between success and failure. Plus, once you've drilled down to that minute level of coaching, if the employee still doesn't succeed, at least you know you've done everything you could possibly do to help.

MANAGEMENT CHALLENGE #6:
WHEN AN EMPLOYEE NEEDS HELP WITH INTERPERSONAL COMMUNICATION

The bad news is that more and more managers tell us that employees are becoming so accustomed to communicating with people electronically, some are losing the ability to communicate well in person. Despite their extensive practice in communicating electronically, a lot of employees are just as bad at e-communication as they are at in-person communication. The good news? Often just the structure and substance of your regular ongoing dialogue with an employee will do much of the work of improving the situation.

What if that doesn't do the trick? If you've been doing regular one-on-ones for several weeks and the structured communication is not teaching the individual better communication habits, then start focusing in your regular one-on-ones on improving the individual's communication habits. Explain: "How you interact with others in the workplace has an important impact. You have room to improve your communication practices. I need you to start working on that, and I am going to help you. Let's start including that in our regular one-on-ones for the foreseeable future."

Over the years we've helped many organizations develop clear standards for interpersonal communication—what I call a "code of conduct"—based on this list of best practices:

- Listen twice as much as you talk.

- Never interrupt or let your mind wander when others are speaking. When it's your turn, ask open-ended questions first and then increasingly focused questions to show you understand what the other person has said.

- Empathize. Always try to imagine yourself in the other person's position.

- Exhibit respect, kindness, courtesy, and good manners.

- Always prepare in advance so you are brief, direct, and clear.

- Before trumpeting a problem, try to think of at least one potential solution.

- Take personal responsibility for everything you say and do.

- Don't make excuses when you make a mistake; just apologize and make every effort to fix it.

- Don't take yourself too seriously, but always take your commitments and responsibilities seriously.

- Always give people credit for their achievements, no matter how small.

I realize that this "code" is a set of very broad performance standards. But you should never underestimate the value of trumpeting them broadly and teaching them in acute instances. You can use this code (or portions of it) whenever you need to evaluate exactly what is wrong with an employee's communication habits. Use the best practices in this code to perform a gap analysis on the employee's communication habits. Identify the gaps and then zero in on your coaching. Start coaching that employee on closing the gap, one best practice at a time.

We've identified the four most common interpersonal communication problems managers identify in their employees:

1. Employees who talk too much at the wrong times
2. Employees who regularly interrupt their colleagues (and you)
3. Employees with bad electronic communication practices
4. Employees who don't know how to conduct themselves in meetings

Now let's take a closer look at each problem and the most effective solutions.

When Employees Talk Too Much at All the Wrong Times

There are two types of overzealous talkers. First, there are the employees who speak up—and don't stop when most people would. These are the individuals who have an opinion about everything and never hesitate to share it. They do way too much of the talking—and not enough listening—in nearly every conversation to which they are a party. They may opine about matters of which they know little or in which they are not involved, or in the presence of big shots who don't appreciate the outspoken underling. The talk-too-muchers also tend to be big conversational interrupters (addressed shortly).

You need to tell them to stop talking so much at all the wrong times. But that lesson usually works a lot better if you teach them what to do instead. Teach them to start listening with much more focus and purpose, to let other people talk, to wait through uncomfortable silences and let someone else break the silence, and to get in the habit of writing down their reactions initially instead of saying them out loud.

Second, there are those employees who always seem to be taking a break. It's hard enough to keep those chatterboxes focused on the work. On top of that, they often distract other employees, drawing them into extra unintended breaks of their own. Sometimes they are merely thoughtless; other times they are actually conniving. Be that as it may, these are the easy cases. Keep the break-takers on task. Hold them to high output quotas. Coach them to replace breaks with more concrete tasks on tighter timetables. Coach others to resist their entreaties. Stop them in the act of distracting others. Keep track of all this in writing. Follow up. And if they don't change their ways, get them off the team.

The harder cases are the very thoughtful and well-meaning employees who nonetheless waste other people's time on a regular basis. Usually this happens inadvertently due to a lack of preparation and focus when it comes to communicating with others: one-on-one, in electronic communication, and in group meetings.

When Employees Interrupt Each Other (and You)

Interrupters come in two forms. First, there are the conversational interrupters. They are almost always the same people as those who talk too much (discussed previously), and they should be dealt with accordingly.

Second, there are the structural interrupters; they try to catch you for spontaneous unscheduled meetings. Surely the antidote to interruptions is regular structured dialogue. When everybody is in the habit of regular, structured one-on-ones, it's much easier to push the interrupters into scheduled conversations. Most people will already have some skill and experience when it comes to playing their parts in those conversations. For those who have a harder time making effective use of one-on-ones, coach them until they start practicing the fundamentals:

- Come in with a clear agenda and a list of updates, questions, and decision points.

- Whenever possible, try to choose a regular time, and stick with it as long as you can. If you have to make a change, try to set a new regular time, and try to stick with the new time as long as you can.

- In-person meetings are always preferable to meetings by telephone, but if your only option is the phone, don't let the phone call slip. And make sure to support these telephone conversations with clear point-by-point emails before and after your calls. Follow-up emails are key, especially following telephone one-on-ones. If you can't follow up with an email yourself, assign this responsibility to your direct report.

- Whenever you can meet in person, try to conduct your meetings in the same place. Choose a good venue, whether it is your office, a conference room, or the stairwell. You want these meetings to become familiar and comfortable. The routine of meeting in the same place every time is an important part of the structure these one-on-one meetings provide.

When Employees Need Guidance in Handling Electronic Communication

Often people sidestep one-on-ones and prefer instead to communicate via electronic message. Electronic communication can be a very powerful tool for effective communication—especially asynchronous communication—but sloppy e-communication practices are every bit as much of a nuisance as sloppy in-person communication. Make sure your direct reports learn and follow good email practices:

- Send fewer and better messages.
- Before sending a message, always ask yourself if this is really something that should be communicated in person at a scheduled one-on-one or a scheduled meeting.
- Send first drafts to yourself.

- If you are "messaging" so you don't forget, then send the "reminder" to yourself too!
- Only cc people who need to be cc'd.
- Use red flags and other indicators sparingly and only when truly warranted.
- Make subject lines smart, and if the topic changes in a reply, update the subject line so it is still relevant; context is everything.
- Make messages brief, simple, and orderly.
- Create a simple folder system for filing incoming and outgoing electronic communication based on how *you* will use them later.
- Establish daily time blocks when you will review and respond to electronic communication, and let people know when to expect your responses.

When Employees Need to Be Taught How to Make the Most of Meetings

Perhaps the most pernicious time-wasting occurs in team meetings, because when time is wasted in a team meeting, the waste is multiplied by the number of people in the meeting. If an employee wastes ten minutes in a meeting of ten people, that is one hundred minutes of productive capacity wasted. Out the window. Youch!! Teach all of your direct reports these guidelines:

- Before attending any meeting or presentation, make sure you know what the meeting is about and whether your attendance is required or requested.
- Identify what your role in the meeting is. What information are you responsible for communicating or gathering? Prepare in advance: is there any material you should review or read before the meeting? Are there any conversations you need to have before the meeting?

- If you are making a presentation, prepare even more. Ask yourself exactly what value you have to offer the group.

- If you are not a primary actor in the meeting, often the best thing you can do is say as little as possible and practice good meeting manners: do not multitask or disturb others with unnecessary noise or activity, and stay focused on the business at hand.

- If you are tempted to speak up, ask yourself: is this a point that everyone needs to hear, right here and now? If you have a question, could it be asked at a later time, off line?

- If you don't have a clear role in the meeting but are required to be there anyway, try not to say a single word that will unnecessarily lengthen it.

MANAGEMENT CHALLENGE #7:
WHEN AN EMPLOYEE NEEDS TO GET ORGANIZED

With the latest electronic devices and systems, how could anybody ever be disorganized ever again? The answer is simple, of course: the greatest devices and systems in the world are no good to someone who doesn't use them. Often there is a disconnect on the front lines between the organizational tools that are available to employees and what they are actually doing.

When managers ask me about dealing with employees who are "disorganized" at work, usually what they mean is that this employee loses track of information. It might be information that is called upon for regular use, will be called upon in the future, or must be passed on to somebody else.

My first question is always, "What system should this person be using?"

I'd say about half the time there is a perfectly good system in place, whether it be high or low tech. The problem is simply that the individual in question is not using the system. He doesn't like it, he doesn't get it, or he never learned it. Often the basic training in using a system has slipped through the cracks for this employee, or maybe the training wasn't very good. Or maybe this employee does not have a particular aptitude for this sort of system. Or maybe the individual in question just hasn't done the work of learning the system and using the system.

Start here, and you will solve half such problems right off the bat: insist that this person get retrained on the system, then follow up in one-on-ones to make sure he is practicing after the retraining and then investing the time in making the transition to using the new system. He may complain along the way, but once he is on the other side of adopting the system, he will reap great benefits from the increased organization. So will you and everybody else who works with him.

A slightly more complicated challenge is when employees are struggling with an information management system that is in place but is really horrible. I've seen this so often: an organization where much of the day-to-day work is tied up in an outdated system that is over-loaded and clunky and does not deliver the optimal functions to users. So people struggle with it, complain about it, and often blame small failures on the system. What do you do? You join the chorus calling for a new system. But you should also ask yourself: Why are some employees much better than others at using the horrible system? Because no matter how bad the system may be, those individuals have mastered it as best as they can, so they get better results from it.

Make sure those best practices are documented by the best practice leaders so they can be taught to others. You need to get everybody up to speed on using the best practices to make the most of a suboptimal system. In your one-on-ones with the weaker users of the system, insist that they start learning and practicing the best practices. Maybe you can get some of the power users to coach the weaker users. You might need to rally the troops to get excited about getting better at using a horrible system.

The good news is that even the worst system is better than no system at all. You can be sure of this: an employee who is disorganized needs to make better use of systems. If there is no system in place for this person to keep track of information, then no wonder he is so disorganized. So how do some employees manage to stay organized on their own? They have come up with their own system for capturing and managing information, I promise you.

If you want to develop new systems, perhaps the first place you should look is the best practices that may have been adopted ad hoc by your more "organized" employees. What systems have they developed that are helping them stay better organized? There may be a way to copy those systems and employ them for everybody else.

Otherwise, you could find yourself working one-on-one with this employee, trying to come up with a system to help this one employee stay organized. If you find yourself in that situation, don't try to reinvent the wheel. And don't try to go from zero to sixty. Focus on the fundamentals.

Managing information is all about storing it for later use. In essence, that simply means keeping track of:

- Information you need to return to regularly (resources)
- Information you need to pass on to someone else
- Information you will need to return to at a specific point

The trickier part of the equation is teaching employees what information to capture and how to capture it so it can be easily managed. That takes practice—ideally, regular practice with the guidance and direction of a good coach. The answers will be different in different situations. You have to figure that out with your direct reports.

Our research shows that when managers instill one very specific habit in employees—note-taking—their organizational prowess increases dramatically, as measured by information tracking error rates. Regular note-taking; doesn't matter if it's on paper or electronic. Whatever the system, when employees are in the habit of taking notes in an organized manner, they get better at knowing what information to capture and how: Before, during, and after one-on-ones and group meetings.

Over time, good note-taking becomes seamlessly intertwined with plans and schedules, to-do lists, and performance tracking. Note-taking becomes part of revising and adjusting work plans and checklists. I often point out that checklists are common in workplaces where there is little room for error: operating rooms, airplane cockpits, nuclear weapons launch sites, accounting firms, and so on. There's a reason: checklists are powerful tools to help people maintain organization and focus.

One of the beauties of working with employees who take notes and use checklists is that you can use those notes and checklists as a tool in your regular one-on-one dialogue with that person. When you get direct reports engaged in this process, you are, in effect, getting them to participate in documenting their own performance by using self-monitoring tools. During your one-on-ones, look very carefully at these notes and checklists, and you will learn a huge amount about where that employee is coming from and where she is going. Use what you learn every step of the way to fine-tune your performance coaching.

MANAGEMENT CHALLENGE #8:
WHEN AN EMPLOYEE NEEDS TO GET BETTER AT PROBLEM SOLVING

Managers often ask me how to deal with employees who are "not good at problem solving." That always makes me wonder: "How many problems come up that truly haven't already been solved before? Why don't your employees have more ready-made solutions to use—at least for the problems that recur on a regular basis—so they don't have to problem solve on the fly?"

Why would you want employees on the front lines to make important decisions on the basis of their own judgment if they could instead rely on the accumulated experience of the organization?

Show me any employee who is making lots of bad decisions, and I'll show you someone who needs to be making a lot fewer decisions, at least for a while. And most of those decisions have already been made. Most "mistakes" in problem solving are decisions that were never up to that employee in the first place. Instead of trying to "make a decision," that employee should have just implemented the ready-made solution—a decision that was already made a long time ago.

Ready-made solutions are best practices that have been captured, turned into standard operating procedures, and deployed throughout the organization to employees for use as job aids. The most common job aid is a simple checklist. Imagine how much better most employees would solve the regularly recurring problems if you were to prepare them in advance:

If A happens, you do B
If C happens, you do D
If E happens, you do F

Many organizations are able to provide not just step-by-step checklists, but automated menu-driven systems. These systems, like checklists, are frequently used in situations where errors could be catastrophic. If you have ever been in a hospital, you have seen these tools in action. Health care professionals are among the most highly educated, highly trained people in the workforce. Yet, rather than just count on their education and training, they are constantly using checklists and menu-driven systems as job aids to make sure they do not deviate from best practices.

As a manager, the question you need to ask yourself is this: What kind of job aids do you have at your disposal to help your employees master best practices for dealing with recurring problems, so they don't have to "problem-solve" anew each time?

If you do already have such job aids at your disposal, then make sure everybody on your team is using them. Go on a campaign. Spread the tools and spread the word. Use them as a centerpiece of your regular one-on-one dialogue with each person until they know the checklists backward and forward and use them without fail.

If you do not already have good job aids at your disposal, then you need to start working with your direct reports to create some!

If several people on your team are doing the same work and facing the same problems, pull them together as a team. Otherwise, take it one person at a time and brainstorm:

- Make a list of every recurring problem you face.
- Taking each problem one by one, ask:
  o Is there an established policy or procedure for this problem?
  o What resources are available?
  o How much discretion will the individual have to improvise? What is the best solution here?
- Spell out a best practice for each problem, step by step.
- Make that spelled-out best practice a standard operating procedure.
- Turn those standard operating procedures into simple job aids, like checklists or automated menu-driven systems.
- Make sure everyone starts using them.

Once you have created these job aids, you will get an enduring return on the investment of creating them. You can use them for training and retraining and, of course, in your regular one-on-one coaching. "Remember, if A happens, you do B. When was the last time A happened? Did you do B? What did you do? If A happens today, then what do you do? Yes, B! Right. OK. Now let's talk about C."

Every step of the way, as you use these job aids to coach your employees, pay close attention. Do the ready-made solutions work?

Can they be improved? Are there permutations and nuances that have come up that the checklist does not anticipate? Job aids should be dynamic living tools that you can revise and improve over time.

Sometimes managers ask me, "Yes, but doesn't this approach actually end-run teaching problem solving? If they never have to puzzle through a problem, how do employees learn to solve problems on their own?"

For starters, they will learn and practice the best step-by-step solutions to as many recurring problems as you can possibly think up in advance. Over time, together, you and they will add more and more recurring problems—and solutions—to that list. Employees who study those best practices and use those job aids will develop a steadily growing repertoire of ready-made solutions. There will be a lot of problems they can solve very well.

"But wait," a manager might protest. "What happens when the employee runs across a problem that was not specifically anticipated? If they are taught to implement ready-made step-by-step solutions, like robots, they won't know how to think for themselves. Won't they freeze up in the face of an unanticipated problem?"

The answer is no. It turns out that by learning and practicing ready-made step-by-step solutions, employees get better not only at solving the specific problems anticipated but also at solving unanticipated problems. By teaching employees to implement specific step-by-step solutions to recurring problems, you are teaching them what good problem solving looks like—like so many case studies.

This is the point at which some managers will say, "I'm sorry, you never really learn unless you face some big problems and make some of your own mistakes. I like to let people learn from their own mistakes." Why not help them avoid making unnecessary mistakes? It is simply nonsense that a good way to learn problem solving is to stumble through problems alone, unguided, trying out solutions based on relatively inexperienced guesses. Why would experience having unsuccessful encounters with problems be a good way to learn problem solving? Experience in solving problems successfully is what comes from learning and practicing ready-made solutions. Employees get in the habit of solving problems well.

In your one-on-ones, when you talk about those ready-made solutions, you have the opportunity to help your direct reports begin to understand and appreciate the common denominators and underlying principles. Talk through with them how they might draw on those common denominators and underlying principles when facing an unanticipated problem. Talk through how they might draw on elements of ready-made solutions, even mixing and matching, to come up with solutions to an unanticipated problem. Talk about how they might extrapolate from ready-made solutions, should the need arise to improvise.

With this approach, you can radically improve your team's—or any individual employee's—record on basic problem solving. You will have fewer problems because anticipated problems with ready-made solutions are not really problems anymore. You will have many more problems that are solved quickly and easily. You will have fewer problems that are mishandled and fewer problems that hide below the surface and fester and grow unbeknownst to anyone.

On top of all that, you will have given your direct reports a strong foundation in the fundamentals of problem solving. On that foundation, they can build more advanced problem-solving skills.

What About More Advanced Problem Solving?

"OK," said one executive in a large engineering firm. "But does this approach actually make employees any smarter?"

I don't know whether you can make anybody any smarter. But I am pretty sure you can teach employees to steadily improve their judgment.

You do not want your employees improvising most of the time. You want them following established procedures. Best practices whenever possible. But it's just not possible to have procedures for everything. You can try very hard to anticipate every situation and help employees prepare. But you can't anticipate every possible situation. There are times when they just have to use good judgment.

How Do You Help an Employee Develop "Good Judgment"?

Good judgment is the ability to see the connection between causes and their effects. Good judgment allows one to project likely outcomes—to accurately predict the consequences of specific decisions and actions. And good judgment allows one to learn from the past; to work backward from effects to assess likely causes, to figure out what decisions and actions led to the current situation.

If you are really trying to help an employee improve her judgment, then start spending time in your one-on-ones discussing with her what she is doing to purposefully and systematically draw lessons from her experiences at work. One day at a time, in your one-on-ones, spend time talking about her day-to-day actions:

Does she think about cause and effect?
Does she stop and reflect before making decisions and taking actions?
Does she project likely outcomes in advance?
Does she look at each decision and action as a set of choices, each with identifiable consequences?

Have you ever played chess? The key to success in any game of strategy is thinking ahead. Before making a move, you play out in your head the likely outcomes, often over a long sequence of moves and countermoves. If I do A, the other player would probably respond with B. Then I would do C, and he would probably respond with D. Then I would do E, and he would probably respond with F. This is what strategic planners call a decision or action tree, because each decision or action is the beginning of a branch of responses and counter-responses.

In fact, each decision or action creates a series of possible responses, and each possible response creates a series of possible counterresponses.

When you are working with an employee to help her improve her judgment, start talking in your one-on-ones about decision or action trees. Teach her to think ahead and play out the likely sequence of moves and countermoves before making a move. Talk it through, play it out aloud together: "If you take this decision or action, who is likely to respond, how, when, where, and why? What set of options will this create? What set of options will this cut off? How will it play out if you take this other decision or action instead?"

Another way to jump-start an employee's growth in problem solving is to teach him to turn his own workplace experiences into case studies from which to learn on an ongoing basis. This is like the case study method that is used by most business schools. Real company cases are presented to students in detail. Who were the key players? What were their interests and objectives? What happened? How did it happen? Where? When? What were the outcomes? Students are then taught to apply the methods of critical thinking to the facts of the case. They are taught to suspend judgment, question assumptions, uncover the facts, and then rigorously analyze the decisions and actions taken by different key players in the case study. The pedagogy is simple: look at the outcomes, and trace them back to see the chains of cause and effect. You can teach employees to apply the case study method to their own experiences:

What actually happened, step by step?

WHEN   WHO   WHAT   WHERE   HOW   WHY

What decisions were made? Who made them? Why? What was the outcome?

DECISIONS   WHO   WHY   OUTCOME

What actions were taken? Who made them? Why? What was the outcome?

ACTIONS   WHO   WHY   OUTCOME

What were the leading alternative decisions that were not made? What different outcomes might have occurred?

*ALTERNATIVE DECISIONS   POSSIBLE DIFFERENT
                           OUTCOMES*

What were the leading alternative actions that were not taken? What different outcomes might have occurred?

*ALTERNATIVE ACTIONS   POSSIBLE DIFFERENT
                           OUTCOMES*

Maybe the most important thing you can do to jump-start your employees' development of advanced problem-solving skills is to teach them to scrutinize their own experiences, both while they are actually happening and afterward. Teach them to stop and reflect, after making decisions and taking actions, as well as when considering outcomes and consequences.

Use your one-on-ones to teach your employees to subject their own decisions and actions to much greater scrutiny every step of the way. What were the specific causes of each outcome or consequence? Help them analyze their own decisions and actions on an ongoing basis.

CHAPTER FOUR

The Challenges of Managing Performance

E ven with direct reports who are mostly on time, well-organized, and regularly following good standard operating procedures, the goal is increasingly "more, faster, better." That's just another way of saying "constantly increase productivity and quality." These are the mantras of continuous improvement. That is the order of the day and will be for the foreseeable future.

It's a lot of pressure. And sometimes managers push back: "Do I really need to be driving people all the time? Constantly nitpicking details? When is good enough performance ever good enough?"

Don't be lulled into thinking that continuous improvement is only about driving more profits and staying ahead (or afloat) in today's fiercely competitive marketplace. Yes, you do need to keep increasing productivity and quality to survive and keep winning. But there are even more compelling reasons to stay focused on continuous improvement with everybody all the time.

Research demonstrates that practicing to get better at something (just about anything) is actually the key to not getting worse. That stands to reason, as human beings are not static creatures. It turns out, if you are not improving at a skill or task, then you are almost surely declining in productivity and/or quality, however slow and imperceptible the decline might be.

It is not so hard to understand and appreciate this dynamic when you consider elite performers. It is obvious that those with specialized skills or particularly challenging tasks must be dedicated to regular, smart, purposeful practice. Nobody wants to be operated on by a surgeon who hasn't performed surgery in a year, no matter how great a surgeon she was a year ago. That's what we mean when we say someone is out of practice. Why do professional athletes practice drills in between games? Why do professional musicians continue to practice scales in between concerts? After all, they are already the best in the business.

Elite performers are so good precisely because they are always working systematically and consistently on trying to get better, almost always with the regular guidance and direction of a coach or teacher or mentor. Elite performers engage in regular, smart, purposeful practice with regular scrutiny and course-correcting feedback from someone they respect and trust. That's why true elite performers always gravitate to strong, highly engaged leaders: they realize they need a coach who knows exactly what they are doing; who is in a position to help them do more, faster, and better; who can get them the recognition and rewards they deserve. If you are not that special someone, most elite performers will find someone else. So if you are managing elite performers on any level, take that lesson to heart. (More on that in Chapter Six, on managing Superstars.)

Strangely, most managers invest most of their performance management time at the low end of the spectrum, coaching low performers aggressively to get them to improve their performance. An employee who develops a track record of failure is the employee most likely to receive significant scrutiny and coaching from his manager. Of course, it is critical to performance-manage the low performers up or out as quickly and mercifully as feasible. But way too many average performers— those who are much more likely to respond favorably to coaching—are neglected as a direct result of all the attention paid to low performers.

Those oft-neglected average employees make up the vast majority of the workforce. They are doing just well enough to escape scrutiny and aggressive coaching, but not so well that they are superstars whom you might be afraid to lose. This is the vast middle—where most of the work gets done—exactly where undermanagement is most likely to hide in plain sight. I see it every day in my work with companies of all shapes and sizes.

The classic case is average employees doing routine recurring tasks. The employee, team, or department seems to be running just fine without much oversight. The employees in question may have been handling the same basic responsibilities for a long time. The work may be low profile, with a relatively small impact on the bottom line. Often the neglect is inadvertent, like so much undermanagement. But sometimes managers do it on purpose, "strategically" neglecting certain employees or teams (or whole departments). The manager might rationalize to himself, "I'm already overworked and underresourced. Why spend my very limited time on aggressive performance management with them?"

There was a large billing group in a medium-sized company with exactly such a manager. I'll call him "Bill." When I first started looking at the operation, Bill assured me, "We have a very simple job, and we do it very well. We do over one thousand transactions a day—entering new customer information, processing electronic payments, and sending out bills. Without us, the company doesn't get any money. So I'd say billing is pretty important." Every time I asked Bill about the performance of the team, he came back at me with "over one thousand transactions a day." That was his key performance indicator. It seemed painfully opaque to me. So I pushed.

When I asked Bill about the accuracy rate on inputting new customer information or updating existing customer information, he told me, "A lot of times sales will send over incomplete information, so that's a problem with sales." What about new customer records that come from internet sales? "Yeah, those come over incomplete too a lot of times. The web team needs to make it so that customers can't complete the transaction without filling in all the information." What about broad measures of billing such as credit cards successfully processed per incoming call? Bill's answer: "We don't track that sort of thing." What about average time to payment? Bill says, "That's accounts receivable." What about the number of customers who go into collection? Bill: "That's collections." What about expired or canceled credit cards successfully replaced? Bill: "That's customer service." And that's how the whole conversation went.

As it happens, I already knew that for quite some time the billing department had been causing headaches for their colleagues in customer service, collections, and accounts receivable, not to mention of late for a couple of people on the web team, and just about everybody in sales. Ask just about anyone in any of those groups where there were problems that affected them, and every one of them said "Billing!"

Billing controlled the secure, proprietary customer database. So whenever billing made a mistake in information transfer, problems would cascade. Customers would call in to ask why they were overcharged, undercharged, never charged, or charged multiple times. Or why their delivery was held up, or came COD. Accounts receivable would be chasing down customers and trying to correct erroneous information in the database. The worst repercussions came from the high number of bills that were going into collection, and of course many customers would be livid, having never received a bill in the first place, or tried to pay repeatedly. Inevitably they would want to talk to the salesperson who had convinced them to buy in the first place, or the sales manager, or the sales manager's manager.

As you might imagine, problems in billing were brought to Bill's attention constantly by other managers (in accounts receivable, collections, customer service, and sales). Don't get me wrong; Bill was not sitting on his hands doing nothing. On the contrary, he was running around like crazy, troubleshooting problems that were constantly being brought to his attention. Meanwhile, he remained incredibly protective of his team, saying things like: "They are the experts at what they do. My job is to empower them and then leave them alone, unless they have problems. When they have problems, I'm there to help solve them. Otherwise, I leave them alone to do their jobs. They are a very senior team with a lot of experience." Indeed, they all had very good performance track records—because Bill had been doing their performance reviews for years.

Bill relished the "empower the team" and "be the troubleshooter" role he had created for himself. It meant he could be friendly in good times and the hero when things got ugly. Rather than being a manager, he was more like the super billing representative. Yes, it meant he had to work a lot. But this was Bill's comfort zone. He just couldn't bring himself to manage the team. For years, he had resisted streamlining the process, defining meaningful performance measures, and managing employees to those requirements.

On the surface, the reported output was fine and the error rates were quite low. But as soon as we looked under the hood, it turned out that the only thing being measured was whether a transaction was successfully completed or a bill successfully sent. There was no meaningful tracking of the true error rate because nearly all of those errors came on the back end of the process. Moreover, once Bill fixed a problem, any record of it would be hidden because the record in question was counted as successfully completed. The only tracking of individual performance was how many records a billing rep took out of the queue and "completed," as well as other automatically captured data such as "ready time" at one's station and "talk time" on the phone or "live time" on chat. These measures were very easy for the individual reps to manipulate. For example, certain of the billing reps would stay "ready" even when they were away from their station, or at the end of a shift they would open a bunch of transactions from the queue and then just close them so at least they took a respectable number out of the queue. (Yes, that caused many problems that would remain hidden until they blew up.) It was a travesty of undermanagement: unnecessary problems were allowed to fester and grow, resources were squandered, and people were doing their basic recurring tasks the wrong way for years on end without anybody noticing.

There were some low performers who had been purposefully hiding out and collecting paychecks. There was a handful of high performers who were wishing somebody would notice them and provide some recognition and reward. More to the point, there were mostly a lot of average performers who wanted to do a good job and were in real need of guidance, direction, and support. Even though they had been doing the same routine tasks and responsibilities day after day—some for many years—they needed help staying focused on continuous improvement, because

1. They were ingraining bad habits through repetition without clear metrics and regular course-correcting feedback. Just because they were doing the same tasks and responsibilities, day after day, does not mean they were doing them right. In many cases, they were doing them just a little bit wrong (or a lot wrong), over and over again.

2. When it came to their mostly repetitive tasks, most of the employees were so comfortable they had grown complacent: "I've done this a million times. It's no big deal. I can do it in my sleep." It does not feel like a challenge, so they put in a tiny bit less effort, and maybe they pay a tiny bit less attention to detail.

3. They had blind spots that had to be pointed out by a manager. Even some employees who were particularly aware, thorough, and self-critical did not know what they did not know.

4. Even some very diligent employees were obviously pushing themselves a whole lot less because they knew nobody was keeping track.

The problem was a fundamental lack of performance management. All the billing department needed was good metrics and regular performance coaching from a highly engaged manager, with some rewards and punishments directly tied to performance.

Bill wanted nothing to do with taking charge of the team and holding them accountable for their performance. When a strong leader was promoted from within, Bill became the "technical expert" and "troubleshooter in chief," a role destined for obsolescence. The new manager and Bill mapped out the billing process from beginning to

end, tightened it up, and created new detailed standard operating procedures for every step in the process. Good checklists and other tools
were created to help the billing reps use ready-made solutions to recurring problems (which was mostly about double- and triple-checking all
information going into the proprietary database):

- If there is incomplete information coming from sales, do A, B, C.
- If there is inconsistent information in duplicate records, do G, H, and K.
- When a transaction clears, verify that it is correct by doing Q, S, and T.

Every record created or changed was attached to a specific billing
rep, and the database was audited regularly for accuracy. As a result,
every billing rep was then managed to a set of clear performance measures directly tied to concrete actions within his control.

The new manager began regular one-on-one dialogues with every
billing rep, focused on those clear performance measures. Those who
met or exceeded their goals were recognized, rewarded, and given
incentives to do even better. Those who fell short were coached to
improve. Those who didn't start improving within a few weeks were
put on performance improvement plans.

It didn't take long for the changes to take root. The low performers had nowhere to hide, and most just left of their own accord. The
high performers got the rewards they had long deserved. Meanwhile,
most of those average performers were glad (at least most days) to work
harder and smarter to do more work faster and better and have the
chance to earn more in the process. Performance improved dramatically: with 20 percent fewer reps, the department increased the number of transactions and brought the real error rate from 21 percent to
under 2 percent. This was a huge relief to all those colleagues in sales,
customer service, the web team, accounts receivable, and collections.
But the real impact on the business was so much greater: namely, all

the customers who would no longer be inconvenienced and angry as a result of wrestling with all those billing problems.

The key to maintaining the high performance levels would be to remain vigilant about ensuring continuous improvement through regular performance management.

Performance Management 101

Employees need to know exactly what is expected and required of them. They also need to know that their performance will be measured based on those expectations and requirements that were spelled out up front—and on nothing else. The key is to always frame expectations in terms of concrete actions the employee can control.

With those measures in place for every employee, the manager needs to monitor, measure, and document every step of the way:

• **Expectations.** Goals and requirements that were spelled out. Instructions given or to-do lists assigned. Standard operating procedures, rules, or guidelines reviewed. Timelines defined. Deadlines set.

• **Concrete actions.** Track each employee's actual performance: What data is tracked automatically? What have you observed the employee doing while watching? What does the employee say when asked about his actual performance? What do his self-monitoring tools reveal? What does your ongoing review of work product tell you? What do you learn about the employee's actions when you ask around?

• **Measurements.** How are the actions matching up against the expectations? Has the employee met requirements? Did she follow instructions, standard operating procedures, and rules? Did she meet her goals on time?

You need a performance tracking process that is simple and easy to use, not cumbersome paperwork that holds you back. Figure out what works best for you.

Most important, tracking gives you the information you need to revise and adjust your regular performance coaching on an ongoing basis:

You did a great job on A, B, and C. You did every item on the to-do list. You followed all the instructions. You followed all the rules. Great job. Now let's talk about D. On D, you failed to complete items 3, 4, and 5 on the to-do list. Why? What happened? Let's talk about how you are going to do items 3, 4, and 5. And now let's talk about E. On E, you missed the following details. Let's go over the checklist and talk about how you are going to fill in those details.

You need to be able to reference your ongoing record of employee performance every step of the way. Make notes before, during, and after every conversation, as necessary. Make notes immediately after the conversation. In between one-on-one meetings, make sure to write down everything of consequence related to that employee's performance. If you think of something you want to mention in your next meeting with the person, write that down.

How Can You Hold Employees Accountable Without Rewards and Consequences?

Often managers ask me: "How do you enforce performance requirements if there are no consequences for failure? How do you incentivize high performance if there are no significant rewards for success?"

It's a whole lot easier to manage performance if you have the resources and discretion (and the guts) to tie specific rewards and punishments directly to concrete actions within the control of the individuals you are managing. Most managers have more discretion and resources than they use, but some managers have very little.

Sometimes all you have is the ability to ask employees on a regular basis to look you in the eye and *give an account* of their actions. Even without rewards and consequences, our research shows that you can have a powerful impact on most employees by simply getting them in the habit of giving a regular account of how their performance lines up with expectations and requirements spelled out in advance. You want them to care about what you think of them. You want them to have a hard time looking you in the eye and saying, after you've spelled out clearly what is expected of them, "No. I didn't do it."

That's accountability: simply getting people to behave as if they know in advance that they will have to explain themselves. Nearly everybody performs at a higher level with regular scrutiny and coaching. The impact is much greater, of course, when the coach brings to the table a high degree of credibility; skill, knowledge, and experience; and a relationship of genuine trust and confidence built over time through regular one-on-one dialogue.

When it comes to your employees, you are the performance coach. That doesn't mean you have to speak with any special dose of charisma or passion, or that you have to suddenly become the natural leader who can inspire and motivate through your infectious enthusiasm. Being the performance coach does mean that you are the one who is talking regularly, one-on-one, with each individual about steadily improving his performance. That's it. If you are the one having that ongoing conversation with each person, then by definition you are the performance coach. On the front lines, ongoing continuous performance improvement means zeroing in on one opportunity after another to improve productivity or quality. By talking about this in your regular one-on-ones every step of the way, you send the message that regular improvement—in productivity *and* quality—is expected: "Speed up here. Fix this tiny problem there. Dot this i and cross this t."

All you need to do is keep talking about the work in a straightforward, effective manner. Your job is to use that bright light of scrutiny to help employees see their targets at work more clearly and aim better at hitting those targets. By shining a bright light on their work, you tell them they are important and their work is important. Best of all, you will help them work a little faster and a little better every step of the way.

The most important aspect of performance coaching is being steady and regular—reliably persistent. Of course, some people have more natural talent than others when it comes to coaching. You will get lots of practice if you are diligent about maintaining your regular ongoing one-on-ones. For starters, just keep talking about the work:

- Focus on specific instances of individual performance.
- Describe the employee's performance honestly and vividly.
- Offer course-correcting feedback.
- Always describe "next steps" in terms of clear expectations: concrete actions the individual can control, with specific guidelines and clear timetables.
- In the next conversation talk about how the actual performance lined up with the expectations set.

You will get better and better at this. You will develop your own coaching voice and style over time. Along the way, you will find that, even without negative consequences, most of the dedicated low performers will want to escape this intensive performance management, so they will leave on their own. And the high performers will do even better with the regular coaching and the recognition that goes along with it, even without additional rewards. Meanwhile, you will help one employee after another practice and fine-tune, become more detail oriented and more aware of the pace of their productivity, develop the habits of continuous improvement, and grow and develop. Doing ever more, faster and better.

MANAGEMENT CHALLENGE #9:
WHEN YOU HAVE AN EMPLOYEE WHO NEEDS TO INCREASE PRODUCTIVITY

Productivity means "output per labor unit." How much work does an employee get done? If an employee doesn't get "enough" work done, then there are only three logical possibilities: that employee needs to work either more, faster, or both.

Simple, right? Just keep that employee in his chair and keep a fire lit under it.

But it's rarely quite so simple. Let's assume you are already coaching your employees as needed on the fundamentals of self-management, so your direct reports are already tuned in to living by a schedule and working a plan. (If not, then *stop* and go back to Chapter Three.)

Managers often ask me, "What about the employee who is in his chair working all day but just seems to work very slowly? How do you help that person speed up and start working at a faster pace?"

Here's what usually happens: Assuming you have metrics in place, the manager shows the employee the numbers and says, "Your number is short of your goal." The numbers are essentially a performance quota: how many units an employee is expected to produce in a certain period of time. It could be the number of data entry records completed, outbound telephone calls made, boxes moved, or widgets manufactured. Let's say an employee is expected to do 120 units in an eight-hour day. That's fifteen units an hour. That's one unit every four minutes. Those are the numbers. If the employee is doing only eighty units in a day, then his productivity is too low. In effect, he is working too slowly. So the manager, metrics in hand, keeps having the same conversation over and over with the employee: "Your numbers are short of the goal. You have to hit 120 units a day. That's fifteen units an hour. That's one unit every four minutes." And the employee says, "Yes, I know. I'm trying." Until the next week, when they have the same conversation again. This is what I call "staring at the numbers together." It's as if some managers are hoping they can *will* the numbers to go up by staring hard enough. At this point, most employees are thinking, "I would like to increase the numbers too. What I need to know is *how* to increase the numbers."

Metrics are great. But they are only step one in performance management. Staring at the numbers would be like a sports coach running down the field alongside a runner, saying "Run faster, run faster." The runner is already trying to run faster. What the runner needs to hear from the coach is *how* to run faster, in the form of good course-correcting feedback: "Pick your knees up. Push off hard. Reach with your stride. Pull your shoulders back. Tuck your chin. Pull your elbows in." And the runner thinks, "Aha! That's *how* to run faster. Now that helps me."

You are the performance coach. The metrics are valuable only if you use them every step of the way to develop good course-correcting feedback for your employees. You need to be able to coach your employees on how to get their work done faster.

First, take a step back: faster is not always better. Imagine two employees who are doing the same basic task, but one is doing it twice as fast as the other. I always joke: either the slow one is playing a lot of solitaire or the fast one is sloppy or cutting corners. Let's assume you've already made sure there are no obvious time-wasters like solitaire. Indeed, sometimes it turns out that employees who work at a faster pace make a lot more errors than those working more slowly. Productivity and quality are in constant tension with each other. When employees are careful to dot every i and cross every t and then double-check and triple-check, it usually slows down production. When employees speed up, quality often suffers. Let's go back to the billing department example I just used. Some of the biggest culprits when it came to making mistakes were the billing reps who had the greatest numbers of completed transactions per day. As soon as rigorous quality assurance was in place, their numbers fell significantly.

Take note: some people work slowly because they are trying to be very, very careful. They are concentrating so hard on getting everything just right that they move deliberately at every point. That commitment to quality should be encouraged. The challenge is coaching the very careful employee to maintain quality but also work on speed.

The default solution for most managers in this case is to say: "Your quality scores are great! But your productivity is too low." The quality-focused employee is usually thinking, "Gosh, I'm going as fast as I can go without risking mistakes."

You need to acknowledge that it's a delicate balance between productivity and quality. The good news is that an employee who is that committed to quality is likely to be an engaged learner and open to performance coaching. Tune in to this quality-focused employee's careful, deliberate style. Take a very deliberate approach to helping her speed up. In your regular one-on-ones, focus on the goal of starting to speed up, slowly but surely.

Spend some time with this employee and together conduct a time-and-motion study (described as follows) of each task in question. Taking it one task at a time:

1. Watch the employee do the task multiple times. Break each task into its component steps, and break each step into a series of concrete actions. Then time the whole thing by timing each concrete action that makes up each step that makes up the whole task.

2. Figure out: How long should the task take? Step by step, concrete action by concrete action. Create a time budget for each task, for each step, for each concrete action.

3. Do a micro-gap analysis. Identify the micro-gaps between the time budget and the employee's actual time, step by step, concrete action by concrete action. In these micro-gaps lie the potential opportunities to speed up.

4. Choose one concrete action at a time to accelerate, and take it slowly. What if the employee could speed up just one concrete action per week? Close the micro-gaps one by one. By going one concrete action at time, you will minimize the chances of increased mistakes in the effort to speed up.

Once you've increased the speed of one task, move on to the next task. Every step of the way, remember to monitor the quality of this person's work to make sure it doesn't dip, and acknowledge the continued high quality as her pace speeds up, slowly but surely.

Quality-focused employees are often very gratifying to coach on speeding up because they are earnest, detail-oriented, and know how to work on getting better at something. You just have to get them to focus their attention on the details of going faster.

Beware, though: sometimes what looks like a great attention to detail is actually some kind of obsessive-compulsive behavior. The triple-checking does not add anything other than satisfying the employee. You already know my answer is that if your employee has a clinically diagnosed obsessive-compulsive disorder (OCD), judging or attempting to treat it is none of your business. However, if you have an employee who is working too slowly because he is repeatedly doing unnecessary tasks or repeatedly building unnecessary steps into tasks, then resolving that problem definitely is your business.

One of the beauties of doing a time-and-motion study of every task, responsibility, and project is that it gives you an opportunity to drill down and see not just *what* your employees are doing but exactly *how* they are doing it. You learn so much as a manager about the employee. You learn so much about the work. And in nearly every case, you will probably find at least a few surprises in the details. Just as some employees work slowly because they are so careful to get everything right, there are plenty of employees who work slowly because the way they are doing it is all wrong, a little bit wrong, or somewhere in between.

When it comes to helping an employee speed up, here are the surprises you should be looking for in your time-and-motion studies:

- *Is the employee doing it wrong?* Look at the employee's every action in the process and check it against the very best practices, action by action. Do a micro-gap analysis. Start coaching to fill any gaps.

- *Is the employee doing unnecessary tasks?* Start coaching the employee to stop doing those unnecessary tasks, regardless of what itch they may scratch.

- *Is the employee building unnecessary steps into any tasks?* (I call these detours.) If so, streamline the process, then start coaching others on how to adopt the streamlined process.

- *Is the employee encountering any recurring obstacles that have not been taken into account?* If so, can the obstacles be removed? Or can a ready-made solution be provided to deal with the obstacles when they occur? Start coaching on using those ready-made solutions when the obstacles come up.

When you take the time to study exactly how an employee is doing a task, responsibility, or project, there are only three ways it can go:

1. You may be surprised to find that carefully following the best practices step by step takes longer than you thought.

2. You may find the employee's more time-consuming approach is so good you deem her approach to be the new set of best practices, even if they do take a little bit longer than the old ones.

3. In any case, you will probably identify some very specific opportunities to help this employee improve—and probably speed up. In your regular one-on-ones, start working on those specific goals, one task at a time: step by step; concrete action by concrete action.

MANAGEMENT CHALLENGE #10:
WHEN YOU HAVE AN EMPLOYEE WHO NEEDS TO IMPROVE QUALITY

Quality means "negative error rate per labor unit"—plus, one could argue, "creativity"—but I'll get to that in Challenge #12. For now, let's focus just on quality in terms of error rate. To determine an employee's error rate, you need to ask: How many errors does an employee make in a defined unit of labor? (A unit of labor might be a particular amount of time, a particular quantity of results, or a number of specified concrete actions.)

The first solution to consider when it comes to the employee with a high error rate is retraining. Employees often find themselves charged with tasks and responsibilities for which they've received little or no training. They haven't been given the information to master or the techniques to practice, sufficient to develop the basic knowledge and skill to do the work. If there is a high concentration of employees with high error rates, there is a good chance the training was insufficient. Indeed, even if the training was great, ask yourself, "Can anyone really get really good at anything after just one class?" Retraining will improve just about anybody's performance, at least for a while, simply by refreshing and refocusing, increasing awareness and mindfulness. Not to mention some of those basic bits of knowledge and skill necessary to do the job. Plus retraining sends a message that doing it right really matters.

Maybe the training was so good the first time that you don't need to repeat it. Or maybe you don't have the resources to retrain employees formally in a classroom. But you can have checklists and your regular ongoing one-on-one dialogue. The continuous reminders and reinforcement of performance coaching is a lot like regular continuous retraining.

What is baffling to some managers is the employee who obviously knows exactly what she is doing and still makes lots of mistakes. She knows the task by heart. She's done it a zillion times. Often this is an employee who is so confident in her competence that she moves through the steps of each task almost automatically, thinking she could do it in her sleep. So she sometimes does. And that's when the errors occur.

You need that employee to wake up. Keep a bright light on everything that employee does. Scrutiny alone can have a huge impact on an employee's attention to detail: if I know someone is keeping a close eye on my performance, I am likely to keep a closer eye on it myself.

Scrutiny, though, is only step one. Don't get stuck in another version of staring at the numbers together. Metrics in hand, show the employee her error rate and tell her explicitly, "Too many errors." If the employee says, "Yes, I know. I'm trying," and then next week you have the same conversation, then the wake-up call alone isn't doing the trick. In that case, you need to use the metrics to develop good course-correcting feedback to help the employee figure out how to make fewer errors.

The answer is almost always, "Slow down and think about what you are doing." The metrics should help you zero in on exactly where and when this particular employee needs to slow down and think, at least for now. That may turn out to be a moving target. That's OK— that's the whole point of metrics and coaching.

As you might have noticed, it's often the speed demons who make the most mistakes. This is especially problematic in positions where the basis for performance evaluation and rewards is disproportionately weighted to productivity measures rather than quality. Indeed, quality is almost always harder to monitor and measure than productivity. Tracking quality requires regular auditing of work product, close attention to the details, and plenty of subjective judgment calls.

Quality assurance slows things down, because slowing things down is how to ensure quality. It's a business judgment you have to make— and a delicate balance for you and your direct reports. To strike that balance, they need your constant guidance and direction: "Work on quality this week. Speed next week. Quality again the week after."

Let's say this week you are going to work on quality. In your regular one-on-one dialogue, start focusing on the goal of eliminating recurring errors, one by one:

• Spend some time with this employee and together conduct an audit of her work product. Get inside the metrics, paying very close attention to the details.

• Take it one task at a time. Review the employee's work in progress and completed work product. Watch the employee do the task in question multiple times. Is the employee following a checklist?

• Look at the employee's every concrete action in the process. Check it against the best practices, step by step, concrete action by concrete action. Do a micro-gap analysis. Start coaching to fill the gaps. If needed, take each item on the checklist and break it down into smaller pieces so there is a mini-checklist for each item.

- Every step of the way, make sure the employee is actually using the checklists. Tell the employee: "Mark a check next to each item as completed on the mini-checklist within each item on the checklist." You might even encourage the employee to make notes in the margins of the checklists. Then you can use those notes and checklists as a tool to guide your coaching conversations.

- If the employee appears to be following best practices, start looking for pitfalls. Zero in on exactly where and when the most frequent mistakes are occurring. Try to figure out exactly what's going wrong.

- Choose one concrete action at a time to make error free, and take it slowly. What if the employee could eliminate just one recurring error per week?

- Once you've increased the quality of one task, move on to the next task. And so on.

- Every step of the way, remember to monitor the productivity of this person's work to make sure it doesn't dip, and acknowledge her continued high speed, even as her pace slows down just enough to dot her i's and cross her t's on that checklist.

The fact that checklists slow a person down is one of the best reasons to use them when improving quality. But checklists work only if they are used. When the checklist becomes so familiar that it seems an automatic drill, it can lose its effectiveness as a quality control. Then you need to use your strong coaching voice to keep the checklist alive and meaningful. Change it up a little: Have people start going through each checklist twice, double-checking. When that becomes passé, maybe you need a week of triple-checking. That's because checklists are not just step-by-step instructions, but also tools of mindfulness.

My lifelong mentor and karate teacher Master Frank Gorman taught me this little exercise about mindfulness. He'd say: "Write your name." Then he'd say: "OK. Now write your name, but leave out every other letter." Then he'd say: "I cut out half your work. Why did it take you twice as long?" The answer, of course, is mindfulness. You have to slow down and think about what you are doing.

If you want to slow people down and get them to think about what they are doing, you need to change the process up a little now and then. Keep challenging them to keep it interesting. Focus on speed one week, quality the next. Focus on removing errors from one task this week, another task the next week.

Everybody gets sloppy once in a while. That's why you need to keep your people awake and mindful and focused on the details every step of the way. One person at a time, one day at a time.

MANAGEMENT CHALLENGE #11:
WHEN YOU NEED AN EMPLOYEE TO START "GOING THE EXTRA MILE"

If productivity is about speed and quality is about slowing down to think, then how shall we define "going the extra mile"?

Managers ask me, "What about the employee who does just enough work and does it just well enough and nothing else? How do you motivate that person to go the extra mile"?

This is usually not the "bare minimum" employee, but one who is at least a notch up. The manager wonders of this person, "Why not try just a little bit harder? Why not do just a little bit more?" Instead, the manager should explain this "extra mile" expectation to the employee in question, in concrete terms, as a regular part of their ongoing one-on-one dialogue.

Often managers balk at that advice: "That misses the whole point! I shouldn't have to tell him." I ask them, "Should your employee be reading your mind?"

Managers often say, "I want this employee to fully meet the formal expectations and even exceed them. And then—on his own initiative—to see what else he can do to help, and then—on his own initiative—to do it!" To which I always say, "So why not just explain to them, frequently and enthusiastically, that 'going the extra mile' is the expectation?"

I was having this very conversation with a restaurant manager (I'll call him "Res") in one of my seminars. Res kept insisting, "That's just setting the bar higher. So now the real expectation is the old expectation plus going the extra mile." My response: "That's exactly right! Let's face it. When you complain that your direct reports are not going above and beyond expectations, you are obviously trying to raise the bar. So raise it! Spell out that higher expectation as clearly as possible."

The reason this is not an entirely satisfying response is that when managers like Res complain that their employees don't "go the extra mile," they are really saying they want employees to think of it on their own initiative. Why is that so important? Res offered this example: "Take a busboy. He's setting tables, pouring water, delivering plates, clearing plates all night long . . . One busboy walks by the salad bar and there's a crouton out of place, he cleans it up on his way to the kitchen without ever breaking his stride. Another guy walks past the salad bar over and over again and never notices it's a total mess. Those are just two different kinds of people. How can you teach someone to care?" I've come to realize that this whole "extra mile" thing has deeper implications for some managers. Some managers are trying to get at some constellation of character issues—work ethic, motivation, commitment, energy, or effort.

I say: Don't go there. Why bother? You probably can't teach someone to care, and it wouldn't be appropriate in your management relationship anyway. But you can require that the busboys stop and check the salad bar once every fifteen minutes or so. Some will do it much more diligently than others. In your one-on-ones with the more diligent busboy, provide recognition and reinforcement and rewards if you possibly can. And in your one-on-ones with the less diligent busboy, spell it out again: "Once every fifteen minutes, walk through the salad bar and clean up anything that is out of place. Are you with me? Are you sure? Let's write it down and create a checklist for the next shift." Then follow up in your next one-on-one until that busboy is a salad bar–cleaning superstar or else a former employee.

I asked Res, "Are you sure you want that busboy taking initiative all the time? What if, for instance, the busboy thought a nice way to 'go the extra mile' was to give customers back massages while they dine? Or if he decided it would be nice to give customers free sodas?" For an employee to truly demonstrate initiative, it would have to be completely self-starting action. In that sense, employees would be taking initiative only when they are doing things that were precisely not expected of them. Surely, sometimes those would be wonderful unexpected things, but sometimes they would likely prove to be not such great initiatives after all. Take a step back, do you really want to teach employees to take initiative by getting them to focus on doing things that are precisely not what's expected of them?

Here's what Res and I worked out: An "extra mile" list for busboys. What would be all the ways that a busboy, doing his job as best he can, could take those extra moments in between his other tasks and add some real value by doing something above and beyond? The list included mostly "area patrols"—like the salad bar. But there were other items on the list. And Res made an "extra mile" list for waiters, kitchen staff, and greeters. He rolled it out to the team, and they ran with it. Res worked with every team to develop an "extra mile" list. Then Res and his assistant managers started including "extra-mile-ism" in their regular coaching. They made it fun and attached prizes and rewards for "excessive extra-mile-ism." Within just a few weeks, Res sent me an email saying, "Everyone is caught up in 'extra-mile-ism'—trying to outdo each other. We are climbing over each other to do more. It's a big win."

Instead of wishing for employees to meet a bunch of unspoken expectations, let people know exactly what it would look like for them to go the extra mile in their particular roles.

Start talking about going the extra mile in your regular one-on-one dialogues:

1. **Make an "extra mile" list for yourself.** What would it look like for you to go the extra mile in *your* role? After you do your job

very well, very fast, all day long. In those extra moments. What are some extra ways you can add value? This will give you a bit of perspective.

2. **Ask every one of your direct reports to make an "extra mile" list for himself.**

3. **Review each employee's "extra mile" list.** Perhaps talking through it together you will both learn a few things. Sometimes managers are surprised to find that items on the employee's "extra mile" list would have been on the manager's list of basic performance expectations. Together, create a working "extra mile" list for that employee. Remember, this is always a work in progress.

4. **Encourage employees to keep score for themselves on how often they complete items on the "extra mile" list.** Take note of those who do and those who don't score a lot of "extra mile" points. For those who do, provide recognition, reinforcement, and rewards whenever you can. For those who don't, ask once in a while, "Why not?"

By making the opportunity to go the extra mile concrete, you give a lot more people the chance to excel in ways they might not have ever come up with on their own. They might not ever have realized it was something they could do or should do, or that you actually expected them to do. Now you are telling them, "These are concrete opportunities to excel. Go get 'em!"

MANAGEMENT CHALLENGE #12:
WHEN YOUR EMPLOYEES ARE DOING "CREATIVE" WORK

If performance management is all about driving continuous improvement in productivity and quality—and helping employees strike a balance toggling back and forth between speed and mindfulness—then where does "creative" work fit into the puzzle?

What is creative work, anyway? If a mason lays one brick on top of another until she has built a wall, has she not created the wall? Yet somehow a distinction is being made between that sort of creating and creative work, per se. If the mason had also designed the wall, we would be more inclined to say the design work is creative—and even more inclined still if the mason had designed a wall that was different from the typical wall. This is what we mean when we talk about creative work: It is new and comes from the imagination; it is the expression of an idea, the more original the better.

We know that creative work can be extremely valuable. But how can you possibly performance-manage creativity? How long should it take to come up with an idea? How do you measure whether or not the idea is good, very good, or excellent?

We typically think of artists, entertainers, writers, inventors, and designers as creative. The truth is that there is always the potential to inject creativity into almost any task, responsibility, or project—into any action. In my view, one could get creative about digging a ditch, if the ditch digger had the right circumstances, inspiration, and support. Of course, the ditch still has to be dug. And that's always the rub.

There are always parameters. A longtime television industry veteran (I'll call him "Tele") once told me, "Take the writers on a situation comedy. They are engaged in a highly creative process. But they have to keep each teleplay inside the twenty-four minutes. They have to work within the characters and back story of the show. At the end of the day, they need to get a show written, and then write another one, and then another."

Yes, some jobs are more creative than others. But even the most creative jobs have three elements in common with other work:

1. A goal (purpose, required outcome, or at least a desired result)
2. A time frame (or an intended structure)
3. Parameters

If you are managing people whose work does not include these three elements, then I've got only this advice for you: Let your great artist create and let the market decide. For everyone else, when you are managing creatives, these three elements are your toolkit.

The biggest favor you can do for employees doing creative work is to keep reminding them of all the stuff that is not within their creative discretion. Tele told me: "You can't sit on the writer's shoulder and nag: 'Write, write, write. Create, create, create.' That doesn't inspire. But it helps them a lot when you remind them we need a story with a beginning, middle, and end. We need a main character to want something and then be denied it, and then try even harder to get it and nearly miss, and then finally get it or not. We need other characters to get in the way or help, on purpose or inadvertently." That's the desired outcome. "It helps them a lot when you remind them it's four six-minute acts: Act I, Act II, Act II, Act IV. It's Act I, scene 1, two minutes." That's the structure and timeframes. "It also helps them a lot when you have established characters: There are four main characters you are writing for, and they are established characters." Tele joked that on the old show *My Favorite Martian*, a popular refrain among the writers was, "A Martian would never say that!" There are the parameters.

Sometimes you as the manager may not have a clear goal. Yet. So you are sending this employee on a creative goose chase of sorts, an exploration. You are asking the employee to "take a crack at it" through wild improvisation to just "see what happens." Maybe this is part of your own creative process: you want something to look at, something that might help you imagine what the goal really should be. If that is what you are doing, then you need to be very clear about that with yourself and with the employee from the outset. Explain exactly what you have in mind, include the employee in your creative process, and explain exactly what role you have in mind for the employee in the process. That's how you avoid this situation: the employee misunderstands, thinks of the process as his own creative process, and then feels like you the manager are failing his creative effort or else hijacking it for yourself. This can leave the employee feeling like his work and efforts have been for nothing. Make it vividly clear to the employee what you do know about the assignment and what role you want her to play in it. Tell her, "I don't know what I'm looking for yet. I'm asking you to help jump-start my creative process. I am asking you to come up with a rough draft, which I will probably send back to the drawing board several times. It is likely that at some point I'll take over the project and rework it myself. Why don't you take two days and see what you come up with?" Now you have a goal, a time frame, and parameters.

In regular ongoing one-on-one dialogue with your creative employees, or when discussing the creative aspects of an employee's work:

1. Remember that parameters, timeframes, structure, and clear desired outcomes are gifts to anybody doing creative work. At the outset of a creative project, it can seem like anything is possible and everything is on the table. That's daunting because it makes the creative process into one agonizing choice after another. Always make it clear what is not within the creative employee's creative discretion.

2. Don't let the creative employee mistake "reinventing the wheel" for real innovation. Make sure that the creative employee is well-versed in all the current best information and best practices on the matter in question before ever trying to invent something new. Real innovation builds on, rather than ignores existing knowledge and skill and wisdom.

3. Whenever the creative is stuck or needing guidance, go back to the desired outcome, parameters, time frames, and structure. Take them one by one. Desired outcome: start with the purpose and then describe as much of the desired outcome as you possibly can—all the details that the creative does not have to create. Parameters: spell them out. Time frame and structure: break it down, so employees understand exactly what is expected of them.

4. Remember, a rough draft is sometimes a good jump-start for the creative process. Encourage your creatives to do rough drafts,

first drafts, second drafts. Rough drafts take the pressure off at the outset and then give the creative and you something to work from and talk about, if not exactly measure.

MANAGEMENT CHALLENGE #13:
WHEN THE EMPLOYEE YOU ARE MANAGING KNOWS MORE ABOUT THE WORK THAN YOU DO

It is not at all uncommon to find yourself managing people whose work you are not sufficiently expert in to manage substantively.

Managers ask me, "How can I set expectations for, much less evaluate, the performance of an employee who knows much more about the work than I do?"

Of course, the employees you are supposed to be managing may find this situation maddening: "How can you be in charge of me when you don't have the knowledge, experience, understanding, or skill necessary to do my job?" That doesn't make your job any easier.

How does this happen? Four ways:

1. The most common scenario is the case of the manager who simply delegates to an employee an area of responsibility—such as a customer account, an internal process, or resource—and over time the employee becomes the in-house expert when it comes to that responsibility.

2. Many organizations have separate management and technical career tracks. Those on the management track get further and further away from their technical background, ironically getting more responsibility and decision-making authority as they become more rusty on technical matters.

3. The manager might be responsible for a cross-functional team in which each employee has a different area of expertise: for example, a software person, a hardware person, an engineer, a finance person, and a marketing person. How can one manager have expertise in all of those areas?

4. The manager may have one or more team members who play particular roles that are tangential to the rest of the team, such as "the computer guy" or the bookkeeper.

You have an expertise gap. The challenge is establishing yourself as a credible performance coach to an expert when you are not yourself an expert. How do you develop meaningful performance metrics and put yourself in a position to provide regular course-correcting feedback?

Step One: start learning. You don't have to become an expert on the work that person is doing. But you do have to learn enough to manage that person. How do you learn? First and foremost, you will learn by managing that person closely over time. Sometimes you have to shadow the expert for a while. Watch him work. See what he actually does and how. Get curious. Read. Watch video. Ask a lot of questions. You don't have to become a doctor to learn a whole lot about a particular medical condition, what to expect, what are the best treatments, what is the best self-care protocol, and how and when will we know if the treatment is working as expected. When it comes to managing your expert employees, learn like you care.

Step Two: every step of the way, think of yourself as a shrewd client and the employee as a professional you've hired. If you are managing a "professional" then you need to know what the professional and industry standards are for performance: What are the professional standards and the established best practices? What data is available on the individual's performance? Is data captured on an ongoing basis? Are there self-monitoring tools that the expert uses to track her own performance? Is there a peer review process to which your expert is subject? If not, how can you begin to monitor and measure and document the expert's actual performance against those professional standards and best practices?

Step Three: if you are going to have experts working for you, then you need to make sure they are high performers, or at least aspiring to be so. You can't have low performers on your team whose work you don't really understand. You want them working systematically and consistently on trying to get better. The challenge is to be their coach when you are not expert in their field.

In your regular ongoing one-on-one dialogue with your expert employees:

- It's OK that you don't know or understand everything the person is doing. But it's not OK to remain in the dark and trust. Keep doing your own research and self-education. And make it clear to your expert that you are on a learning path.

- Focus on desired outcomes. Be a smart, assertive, careful patient or client. Ask good probing questions every step of the way. If you don't understand the answers, say so. Ask more questions. Don't allow yourself to be brushed off. Get a second opinion—and a third.

- Engage the expert and make him complicit in spelling out expectations. Ask for details: "Exactly what are you going to do? Why? How are you going to do that? Why? What are the steps? What is involved in each step? How long will each step take? Why? What are the guidelines and specifications?" If the answers are vague, press for more details. If the answers are complex, ask for explanations a lay person can understand.

- Every step of the way, make reference to professional standards and established best practices and ask how the expectations being spelled out and the actual performance being measured align.

- As you monitor and measure performance, stay focused on the desired outcomes, the expectations the expert has helped spell out, and the standards and best practices. Use any and all data that is automatically captured about the expert's performance, and ask the expert to help you understand the data. Engage the expert in using self-monitoring tools. Look at the work product and keep asking questions: "Did you do what you said you were going to do? Why or why not? How did you do it? How long did each step take? Why?"

- Make a point of comparing experts doing similar work to find patterns of similar practice and deviations. Talking to multiple experts doing similar work is also a good reality check, so one expert can't easily pull the wool over your eyes.

• Don't forget to ask around for additional soft data. Ask customers, clients, vendors, coworkers, and other managers. Get those second and third opinions whenever you can.

• Every step of the way, document the fundamentals of your conversations. What expectations were established? How did the performance line up with the expectations? As you are documenting performance, ask the expert employee to tell you what she thinks you should document and why.

Over time, you may never become an expert, but you will know more. You will get to know the person's work better, as well as his work habits and track record. You will be better able to gauge the employee's veracity, trustworthiness, and reliability. You will be able to tell whether the person is on or off track. You will be able to read the conversations you are having by the way the person talks and the kinds of things he says. Certainly, you will learn enough to hold that person accountable to clear metrics and provide regular ongoing course-correcting feedback, keeping that person on a track of continuous improvement toward elite performance.

CHAPTER FIVE

The Challenges of Managing Attitudes

If you are like most managers, you avoid dealing with employee attitude problems, even though you know that employee attitudes matter a lot. Attitude affects productivity, quality, and morale. It also has a huge impact on collegiality, cooperation, and cohesion. It can be the difference between employees embracing or rejecting development opportunities. Attitude can make the difference between retention and turnover. Good attitudes drive positive results. Bad attitudes put a drag on results.

So why do most managers avoid dealing with bad attitudes? Avoid it, that is, until they can no longer be avoided? By then it is too late, and the conversation is doomed to become a difficult confrontation.

Attitude is hard to talk about for three basic reasons:

1. It seems so personal—like maybe it's none of your business.
2. It seems intrinsic to the person, so probably impossible to change. That's why people say things like, "That's just who he is."
3. It seems intangible, so it is hard to describe in clear terms. You might think, "She is doing her job, after all. Who's to say she has to do it with a smile on her face all the time?"

That's why most managers mostly avoid giving employees negative feedback about attitude unless the behavior is truly egregious. Unless bad behavior is so incessant that even you can't take it anymore, you probably let most of the behavior slide. Sometimes you might make an offhand comment, a hint, a suggestion. And you don't push too hard, because those with bad attitudes are also the most likely to take offense. Telling an employee he has a bad attitude is a good way to make a bad attitude even worse. When you do let it slide, those with "good attitudes" typically work around it just fine. This sort of thinking is how bad attitudes become accepted and absorbed into the fabric of the workplace, putting a drag on performance while hiding in plain sight.

You (or a colleague) might offer a periodic reproach to those with bad attitudes, usually delivered lightly and in passing, which means the behavior is barely pushed below the surface. When it recurs, it might escape your notice. Or it might just slide by again, or it might be reproached again, maybe lightly and in passing, or greeted by coworkers with the routine murmurs of disapproval. Unless it pops up just one too many times, or at the wrong time, or with the wrong person, or it comes out just a little too much or a little too loudly. Then perhaps there is an outburst or an exchange of words—or worse.

Whenever you get the guts to address the matter—even if it seems like a time when cooler heads might prevail—it can be very hard to find the right words. The "attitude" in question may seem intangible, hard to measure in objective terms, so descriptions of that behavior may seem subjective: "You seem unfriendly"—or negative, unhappy, angry, frustrated, or "fill in the blank"—can all receive the retort, "No. I am *not*." That's because they are all statements about the individual's inner state. And who is better qualified to comment on that person's inner state than that person? Certainly not you, that person's manager, unless you are a licensed psychological therapist.

Meanwhile, trying to describe an employee's attitude—especially when that person is not at his or her best—is likely to provoke an emotional response from the employee. The employee may well feel attacked. The criticism may come as a shock, as if without warning, especially when the employee has been behaving this way for some time. The employee may well say (or think), "This is a personal attack. It's just who I am. Are you asking me to change my personality?"

This might in turn provoke an emotional response from you, the manager. You might think (or say): "I've been putting up with this nonsense for way too long. I've had just about enough. Maybe who you are is not the right person for this job!" That's how a conversation quickly hits a downward spiral.

That's why most managers tend to second-guess themselves on issues like this, thinking: "Maybe this issue is too personal. Is it even something that this person can change?" No wonder you avoid dealing with employee attitude problems.

Feelings Are on the Inside; Attitude Is What You Do on the Outside

I've been throwing around the term "attitude" here for several pages now. What exactly is "attitude," anyway? This question is a bit like the U.S. Supreme Court consideration of pornography, in which Justice Potter Stewart famously wrote (here I paraphrase) "It is hard to define, but I know it when I see it."

I use the term "attitude" to zero in on that very special category of employee performance problem that matters so much but seems so hard for so many managers to actually get their arms around. As long as you think of attitude as a personal, internal matter, it is going to remain intangible, and you will remain out of your depth. Plus, whatever your employees may be "feeling inside" is indeed none of your business. Stop focusing on the inside/personal stuff. Focus on the outside.

Feelings are on the inside. Observable behavior is on the outside. That observable behavior can be seen, heard, and felt. When we talk about attitude, it's not about who the person is, it's about how the person behaves. No matter how intrinsic the source may be, it is only the external behavior that can be and must be managed.

Attitude Is Expressed in Communication Practices

If you focus on that observable external behavior, all of a sudden it becomes really simple. On the outside, attitude is all about communication practices: Words, format, tone, and gestures.

Just like any other aspect of performance, the only way to lead, manage, or supervise employee attitude is with strong, highly engaged management. That means steady, consistent, high-quality communication—your only real leadership tool—high structure, high substance. It's just a matter of applying the fundamentals to this difficult, complex, and all-too-common challenge. You need to define it and spell it out as a set of expectations, and then monitor, measure, and document it—require it, recognize it, and reward it—like any other aspect of performance.

Do you want to be great at dealing with employee attitude problems? Do you want to find it downright easy to tell employees when and how they need to change their attitudes at work? Here's what you need to do:

- **Don't let attitude be a personal issue.** Instead, make it 100 percent business. Make great attitude an explicit and regularly discussed performance requirement for everyone. Make it all about the work.

- **Never try to change an employee's internal state; speak to only the external behaviors.** It's not about what the employee is feeling deep inside—the source of the attitude issues—but rather what the employee is expressing on the outside. External behavior is something an employee can learn to perform, and it is something you can require.

- **Refuse to allow attitude—great, good, or bad—to remain vague in any way.** Make it 100 percent clear. Define the behaviors of great attitude: words, tone, and gestures. Spell it out. Break it down. Monitor, measure, and document it every step of the way. Talk about it. Hold people accountable. Reward the "doers." Remove the "won't-ers."

Yes, You Can Require Great Attitudes at Work

Great attitudes in the workplace add directly to the bottom line. There is no doubt about that. How can you require people to have great attitudes?

Back in the 1990s we did some work with a huge grocery store chain. They got a lot of publicity because of a customer service initiative that included requiring retail employees to "smile and make eye contact" when they encountered a customer in the store. Some employees said, "How dare they tell me I need to smile and make eye contact?!" As you might imagine, they were overwhelmingly the ones with bad attitudes. Those with great attitudes typically said, "Well, of course I would make eye contact and smile when I encounter a customer! Anyone who wouldn't really shouldn't be working here." There was indeed a spike in turnover. There was also a great deal of training and coaching up and down the chain of command. After only a few months, the vast majority of employees were in favor of continuing the initiative, including those still employed who had been uncomfortable with the requirement at the outset. The customer service and overall customer satisfaction ratings shot through the roof in virtually every store where the initiative was successfully implemented.

Maybe this story is an extreme example of zeroing in on specific communication practices to drive great attitude behaviors. But it is highly instructive. Great attitude behaviors should be—at a bare minimum—treated as one among many very important basic performance requirements. Some organizations make great attitude behaviors a centerpiece of their entire workplace culture. It's really all about professionalizing workplace interactions for greater collegiality and cooperation. This has a huge impact because it takes the attitude issue out of the shadows and puts it squarely into the day-to-day conversation about performance. It is a regular reminder to people to keep smiling on the outside, if you will, regardless of what is going on deep inside.

There Are No Bad Employees. Only Bad Behavior

What about the ones who have a hard time consistently smiling on the outside?

Even people with overall great attitudes have their moments. So the broad performance standards and regular reminders in one-on-ones really make a difference, even for them. Of course, some people have more trouble than others maintaining a positive attitude. You don't need to write those people off. But you can't tolerate anything less than great attitudes.

Communication practices are habits. Habits can be changed, but it isn't easy. The only way to shift from a suboptimal habit to a much better habit is through the consistent, disciplined practice of a proven technique over time. The proven technique functions as a replacement behavior. At first it is very hard. But it gets easier and easier over time. And eventually the best practice becomes a new and much better habit.

Early on in my work, I met a very dedicated health care administrator I'll call Beth. She had a rock-star skill set, and her boss (the health care system CEO who was my client at the time) wanted her on his executive team, but her communication style was really getting in the way. The CEO asked me to spend some time coaching Beth.

Beth went into nearly every conversation entirely straight-faced and tight-lipped. She would talk through a printed one-sheet she had prepared for each meeting and then offer short, focused responses to the other person's agenda items. Beth was all business. So far, not exactly warm and fuzzy, but perfectly fine.

What was the problem? Beth did not suffer fools, and she had a way of manifesting disapproval—almost disdain—that really rubbed people the wrong way. Beth had a signature response that occurred way too often: she would fold her arms, roll her eyes, and say, "No." To be clear, this was usually not in response to a yes-or-no-question. Her boss or a colleague or a direct report might begin to share a piece of information, explain how a particular project was being organized, or ask an open-ended question like "What is your plan for a, b, c?" In response, Beth was likely to just fold her arms, roll her eyes, and say, "No." Then she'd just wait. It was very off-putting.

I asked Beth if she was aware that some people thought she had room to improve her communication style. She was aware. I asked her what she thought she could do to improve. Let's just say that didn't go too far. So I decided to zero in on her signature response. I said: "Beth, let me give you an example. I don't know if you realize that you have a very off-putting habit. When you don't like what you are hearing, you often fold your arms, roll your eyes, and say, 'No.'"

As if on cue, Beth folded her arms, rolled her eyes, and said, "No." That was all it took. We just sat there for a minute and she said, "What do you want me to do?" I said, "Something else! Anything, really." We chuckled, and that broke the tension.

Then in all seriousness I gave her my very best advice. I told Beth she needed to adopt a replacement behavior. She needed to train herself to behave differently when she felt that signature response coming on. I suggested opening her arms wide, smiling wide, and saying, "Yes. Please tell me more about that."

Like I said, Beth was all business. She practiced the new technique with discipline and made it into a new habit. In the process, she became much more aware of her communication practices in general. Beth identified additional communication habits she wanted to change, and she used the same approach—replacement behaviors—to change those habits. One by one, she replaced her suboptimal communication practices with much better ones. Within a very short time, with discipline and focus and a little bit of coaching, Beth radically improved her communication style in a way that made her a much more valuable employee. That was a great outcome for Beth, for every person with whom she worked, and for her employer!

Very few employees are like Beth. Most need a lot more guidance, direction, support, and coaching to make a meaningful change in any habit, much less something as sensitive as their communication practices.

Sad to say, some attitude problems will resist solutions even when you deal with them meticulously, aggressively, and persistently. Maybe it really is a problem on the inside, one that nobody can ever help that employee fix. At some point, the only place to go is to let that employee know that his job is on the line. Whether or not, and when, to fire an employee is always a tough decision. But sometimes it just has to be done.

For the vast majority of employees, however, if you have the guts and discipline to coach them meticulously, aggressively, and persistently, they will either get better or else leave on their own.

MANAGEMENT CHALLENGE #14:
WHEN AN EMPLOYEE NEEDS AN ATTITUDE ADJUSTMENT

When an employee starts seeming like someone with a bad attitude, you need to start talking about that in your regular one-on-one dialogue with that person. Zero in on the negative behaviors, one at a time:

1. **Describe the specific words, format, tone, and gestures.** Remember Beth, my previous example: "You fold your arms, roll your eyes, and say 'No.'"

2. **Connect the behavior with tangible work outcomes:** "This makes other people, including me, reluctant to approach you even when they need something from you. Also, when you manifest disdain for someone, that person has an automatic incentive to diminish the weight of your opinion."

3. **Make reference to the performance requirement or best practice from which the negative behavior deviates:** "We all need to be available and welcoming to each other in order to keep each other informed, cooperate with each other, and meet each other's business needs."

4. **Define the replacement behavior** that you will use as a specific performance expectation against which to measure the

individual's improvement. Discuss some possible replacement behaviors and then decide on one, like Beth's replacement behavior of smiling wide, opening her arms wide, and saying "Yes. Tell me more about that."

5. **Continue to follow up in your ongoing one-on-ones.** Pay attention. Monitor, measure, and document as best you can. Ask the individual to self-monitor and report to you on progress on a regular basis. Reward success. Do not accept failure.

The Six Attitudes Most Commonly in Need of Adjustment

It is no doubt true that every case is different, especially if one really tries to understand the inner feelings at the source. The good news is that the inner feelings of each employee are none of your business. Using the outside lens of communication practices, we've identified in our research the six most common types of individual attitude problems—aberrant communication habits—that have a negative impact in the workplace, and we have come up with names for the employees who exhibit them:

1. Porcupines
2. Entanglers
3. Debaters
4. Complainers
5. Blamers
6. Stink-bomb throwers

Porcupines

Lots of people just want to be left alone at work. I usually separate them into the loners, the hiders, and the porcupines. The loners and hiders are not much trouble. They can usually be coaxed out pretty easily by a strong, highly engaged manager who includes them in team meetings and conducts regular structured one-on-one dialogues. They may be less social by nature, more introverted. That's fine. With guidance and direction, they will improve their skills and develop better habits for more engaged workplace relationships.

The porcupines are another story altogether. Porcupines want to be left alone with a special vengeance. Their words, tone, and gestures all say: "Get away from me!" Your entreaties will be greeted, at best, with a cold, curt response meant to discourage further interaction. Or you may well be received with a stinging word, tone, or gesture. After a few times, you learn to keep your distance. That's why I call them porcupines.

It's rarely the case that porcupines are avoiding work. Often porcupines do a lot of work very well, very fast, all day long. They just insist on being "left alone to do my work." That is another way of saying they want to do whatever they think should be done, wherever, whenever, and however they think it should be done. And they don't want to be bothered with anybody else's priorities.

That's just not an acceptable position. Everybody needs to be approachable, welcoming, and professional in their workplace communications. Nobody gets to do whatever they want to do however they want to do it all of the time when somebody else is paying them.

Some porcupines walk in the door every day with their quills up: "Get away from me!" Others are less overt about it. Some would prefer nobody even knew they were there. That's the one who seems like he's been working in the same corner cubicle forever. On what? "Why do you need to know?" He has eyes in the back of his head, waiting for someone to try—just try—to come over and start a conversation with him. Or call. Or send an email.

The most common mistake managers make with porcupines is to "get the message" and keep their distance, approaching rarely and then very carefully. That's what everybody does with the porcupine. She raises her quills because it works.

Don't surrender. Find your guts and get your arms around the porcupines. (Don't worry. That's just a metaphor.) Engage that porcupine in the same regular, ongoing, structured one-on-one dialogue that you do with every other direct report.

That's one of the beauties of having a workplace and team culture of ongoing, structured dialogues. When everybody on your team is expected to have regular one-on-ones, porcupines—just like everybody else—know from the outset that nobody gets to be left alone. Just having that structure in place goes a long way toward taming most porcupines in a matter of weeks. Don't let yourself or the porcupine off the hook.

The one-on-ones with you should also give the porcupine a chance to practice interacting in a more approachable, welcoming, and professional manner—at least with you. As you fine-tune your ongoing dialogue with the porcupine and you both become accustomed to your one-on-ones, you will get into a rhythm. Once they get used to the process, porcupines often prefer this sort of scheduled, organized, and focused communication to more spontaneous interactions. The structure pays off in short order in the form of fewer interruptions. Sometimes porcupines find they prefer the structured communication so much that they start scheduling regular one-on-ones with their most regular "interrupters" and find that they quickly improve their working relationships with those colleagues as well.

What if the structure alone is not enough to solve the porcupine's communication problem? That's when you start talking about it in your one-on-ones: The goal is to help the porcupine use different words, format, tone, and gestures to become more approachable, welcoming, and professional. Zero in on the specific negative behaviors that seem to say, "Get away from me!" and replace them with new behaviors that say, "What can I do to help? Maybe we should schedule a specific time to discuss this. Maybe we should schedule a regular time for an ongoing dialogue?"

Entanglers

The opposite of the porcupine is what I call an "entangler." Entanglers want everybody else to be involved in their issues, no matter how mundane or idiosyncratic those issues may be. As much as porcupines do not want attention, entanglers want to be noticed, observed, listened to, and engaged. It's as if they are lonely and want you to keep them company while they do whatever it is they do. It looks a lot like narcissism if you take it apart—whatever it is that's going on for the entangler at any given point, the entangler just wants you to share in (or be the audience for) that experience.

Don't get me wrong: most people do work that requires ongoing communication and cooperation with coworkers. That sort of interdependency is not the same as entangling, but do beware! Entanglers often disguise their behavior in the claims of legitimate interdependency. Here's how you can tell the difference: true interdependency jocks keep their communications highly purposeful—brief, straightforward, and efficient, almost always focused on concrete next steps. They are always trying to wrap up the conversation. For entanglers, communication is not a means to an end, it is the end itself. Their conversations don't resolve in to-do lists for each party. Their every word is meant to draw you in to further conversation and in-tandem activities.

In tone, entanglers can be positive or negative or somewhere in between—often they vacillate between positive and negative based on whatever will get them the most attention at the moment.

With entanglers, it is often unclear whether or not there is a real issue at stake, because what they seek is entanglement per se. Their issues often remain forever unresolved, because resolution is the last thing they want. Involving others in their thoughts, words, and actions is the goal—an end in itself.

The problem is that entanglers take up too much of everybody else's time and often send others on wild goose chases. Not only that, but after one or more such experiences, often their colleagues start avoiding them. This only makes the entanglers seek attention all the more. They find new people to entangle, who in turn start avoiding the entangler. Plus, whenever the entangler does have a real issue at stake, it's a bit like the boy who cried "Wolf!" So those real issues may be neglected as a result of the entangler's reputation for entangling others unnecessarily.

The most common mistake managers make with entanglers is steering clear of them, like everybody else does. Usually the manager has been drawn in by the entangler many times and has vowed not to be drawn in again. Of course, this only makes the entangler become even more needy. If he can't chase you down, then he starts chasing after the attention of others, perhaps those who are less aware and less wary.

When you engage the entangler in that same regular, ongoing, structured, one-on-one dialogue, all of a sudden the entangler knows for sure he can count on your attention at least once a week. Or maybe it should be twice, three times, or four. Remember, some people need more frequent one-on-ones than others. Entanglers typically need to meet with you more often than others. They need more regular feedback and direction. That's why they keep trying to entangle other people in conversation. You will often find that simply giving the entangler your attention one-on-one for fifteen minutes a day, three days a week, can pay off hugely for you, the entangler, and the whole team.

The one-on-ones should also give the entangler a chance to practice interacting with greater efficiency and efficacy—at least with you. Over time, you will help the entangler learn to prepare better agendas for your one-on-ones; increasingly organized, clear, and focused. In the course of your regular one-on-ones, teach the entangler to prepare in advance a clear agenda—in writing—for every conversation with you.

Teach the entangler how to communicate in a highly purposeful manner—brief, straightforward, and efficient. Teach him to focus on concrete next steps. Teach him how to wrap up every conversation with clear to-do lists for each party.

The entangler will usually begin to realize that efficient and efficacious interactions are far more gratifying than entangling. As the entangler gets better and better at scheduled, organized, and focused communication, he will find his colleagues increasingly willing to give him their attention when there is a legitimate business need.

The goal: help the entangler use different words, format, tone, and gestures to become more efficient and efficacious in his interactions. The method is to zero in on the specific negative behaviors that seem to say, "Crying wolf!" and replace them with new behaviors that say, "I have prepared in advance a clear focused agenda for this conversation. Maybe we should schedule a specific time to discuss this. Shall we schedule a regular time for an ongoing dialogue?"

Debaters

If entanglers are into communication that goes nowhere in particular, debaters always speak as if they have an agenda. Often it's the other side of whatever is being said. But it's not always the devil's advocate point of view. Sometimes debaters have a very specific interest or constituency whose perspective they seek to represent, seemingly in every conversation at virtually every turn. In other cases it might be a different issue every day. But it's always something. The debater always has an argument to make.

It's very good to have employees who can make a good argument. You don't want every employee to be a yes-man. You don't want a team of group-thinkers. You need to have room for a critical perspective so you don't make unnecessary mistakes. You need a free flow of information and ideas so that you can tap into everybody's knowledge and insight.

If you are engaging everybody in regular one-on-ones, then everybody has a natural venue in which to discuss their knowledge and insights on a regular basis. Anybody who has an agenda always has a ready-made forum. Not only that, but that forum becomes a perfect place for debates that are introduced in other conversations or meetings. When they start to raise an argument, just say: "Let's plan to discuss this in our one-on-one on Tuesday at 10 A.M., OK?"

If the issue is in any way complex, ask the individual to prepare an executive summary of her argument in writing to you in advance of your one-on-one:

Here's the issue.

These are the options.

This is the option I propose.

This is why my option is best for the business.

Here's what it would cost—money, time, people, and other
   resources.

This is where we could get the resources.

This is what the plan would look like.

Here's the role I propose for myself in executing that plan.

This gets the debater to really focus. Just how important is this?
And if the answer is "very," then it gives the debater a chance to put
her best foot forward in making the case. If she makes a great case in
your one-on-one, maybe you'll ask her to present the argument to a
larger group.

This is also great training: it's a great way to help debaters (and
anyone else) learn and practice the art of making a persuasive business
case, not to mention refine and develop their greater understanding of
the work.

Meanwhile, by integrating any debater's arguments into your regular, ongoing one-on-one dialogues, you have good quality controls in
place to ensure that you give each argument a good hearing without
allowing arguments to go on forever. The debater feels heard and,
indeed, important countervailing views are not shut down or shut out.
On the other hand, once an argument has been fully made and heard,
then a decision is reached. That means the question is settled. No more
debate unless there is strong new evidence.

As a bonus: You will learn more and more about who has a clear
understanding of the business and who doesn't; who has a knack for
identifying pitfalls ahead; who has good ideas and who has better ideas;
whose ideas are half baked. Maybe you'll learn something valuable
from all those well-presented arguments.

Complainers and Blamers

I treat complainers and blamers together because they are such close
cousins. The most important thing the characters have in common is

that each points responsibility for problems away from himself. Often they work as a sort of tag team: The complainer points out something negative and the blamer jumps in and points a finger at somebody—internal or external.

What's the difference between complaining and troubleshooting? Complainers often complain that they get a bad rap: "After all, isn't it important to point out problems? Are we supposed to pretend that everything is OK even when it's not?" Here's the key difference: Complainers typically make noise about the symptoms of a problem (the pain), whereas troubleshooters go looking for the root cause.

Blamers may retort, in defense of their blaming, "Looking for the root cause is exactly what I'm doing. And the root cause has to be something, or someone. When I point out the root cause, I am tarred as a 'blamer.'" So what's the key difference between blaming and troubleshooting? Here's the key difference: The blamer is focused on who else did something wrong, the troubleshooter is focused on what steps she can take herself to make things better.

Things go wrong in every workplace. No matter how great your work, your colleagues, or your organization, problems are an everyday reality. Mostly these problems are probably not caused by the complainers and the blamers. And it is plenty likely that neither the complainer nor the blamer will be in a position to correct many of the problems which might well have an impact on them.

That's one of the prime frustrations for most people in the workplace: It's easy to identify problems, but not so easy to solve them.

The regular one-on-ones are a natural venue in which everybody can raise points of pain on a regular basis and work with you to either move toward a solution or create a coping mechanism. Ask the complainers and the blamers both to keep a running list of pain points. You can always defer complaining and blaming to the running list and make time in your one-on-ones for discussion. When they start to complain or blame in any other conversation or meeting, just remind them: "Add that to the list and let's make time to discuss that in our next one-on-one."

Just as with the debater, it's a good idea to ask the complainer/blamer to lay out her case in writing:

Here's the point of pain.

Here's why it's bad for the business.

This is the root cause.

These are the options for a solution.

This is the solution I propose.

This is why this solution is best for the business.

Here's what it would cost—money, time, people, and other resources.

This is where we could get the resources.

This is what the plan would look like.

Here's the role I propose for myself in executing that plan.

This is a great way to get a complainer or blamer to consider: Is this a serious point of pain?

The most common problems you tend to hear about from complainers and blamers are not emergencies, or anything special, for that matter. They are usually small mistakes, omissions, and inconveniences that occur in the regular course of business. No problem is so small that it should be left alone; small problems too often fester and grow into bigger problems. So jump on the complainers' and blamers' unfailing eye for even the smallest points of pain and constantly reiterate the expectation: "Whenever you diagnose a problem, no matter how small, go into troubleshooting mode. Take responsibility. Focus on finding the root cause and focus on what you can do to try to fix it."

You do want to hear about it when things go wrong, but always in a professional, productive manner. Talking about small problems—whatever they may be—should be something you do as a matter of course in your regular one-on-ones anyway. Addressing one small problem after another is what ongoing continuous performance improvement is all about.

Teach the complainers and blamers to be troubleshooters—a great metamorphosis for everybody involved. It's always a good thing to have more troubleshooters on the team.

Stink-Bomb Throwers

Everybody gets angry sometimes. Some are more apt to show discontent than others. Some people go as far as making sarcastic (or worse) remarks, cursing under their breath (or aloud), or even making a loud gesture such as slamming a door (or their hands down on a table). This sort of "communication" is what I refer to as a "stink bomb." It's basically just a tantrum.

Like the blamers and complainers, the stink-bomb throwers (SBTs) are aware of a problem—they are feeling some pain. The thing about SBTs is that they are usually angry.

The most common mistake managers make with SBTs is to write them off. Expressions of anger are disturbing, so we tend to treat them as illegitimate.

But anger is data. So it bears investigation. So the first part of the solution to the SBTs is to pay attention to the data. Don't pretend it didn't happen. Focus on it like a laser beam: "Mr. SBT, you just slammed your hands on the table. That tells me you are seeing something wrong here." Then take the same approach as the one outlined for the complainer or blamer. Ask him to prepare a brief in writing about the issue and plan to discuss it in your one-on-one.

The problem is, SBTs are apt to respond by saying something like, "No. Everything is fine." That's because throwing the stink bomb is sometimes just a way of letting off some of the steam, and now they have it under control again. They've made it clear they are not happy. They've soured the mood a little for everyone. Now they are ready to go back to seething within.

You can't allow the SBT to squirm away from the consequences of his tantrum. Be very clear: "Everything is not fine, because you slammed your hands on the table. I have a responsibility to treat that as important data." Then return to the issue in your next one-on-one.

You cannot ignore the data, and you do need to shut down this behavior. Anger is like a drug—fight or flight generates some serious brain chemistry. When you are dealing with angry people, it's like dealing with people who are on some bad drugs. As with any bad attitude, you as the manager cannot treat anybody's anger in the workplace. Don't try! If anybody in the workplace is overtly expressing anger in verbally or physically inappropriate ways, that is simply external behavior that you simply cannot tolerate in the workplace. So you need to remove this person or fix the behavior. (Or, if the person is uniquely valuable, find a way to isolate him from the rest of the team.)

This is a case where you might try dedicating some one-on-one time to aggressive coaching on behavior modification.

Instead of saying, "You need to express yourself in a more professional manner and refrain from having temper tantrums in the workplace," try saying something like this:

- **Describe the problematic behavior**: "Three different times in our team meeting yesterday, you slammed your hands down on the table and said quietly but audibly, 'This sucks!'"

- **Explain the impact on work**: "This is distracting to others, intimidating, and it does not get any meaningful information on the table to identify a problem or move toward a solution."

- **Spell out the behavior you want to see instead**: "The next time you feel inclined to lift up your hands to slam them on the table, instead I want you to pick up a pen with one hand and a piece of paper with the other. Make a note to yourself. And the next time you feel inclined to say 'This sucks!' or anything like that, instead I want you to smile and say 'Golly.' And if you can't bring yourself to do that, then just bite the back of your tongue. Right side or left side of the tongue—either way, that's totally up to you."

Make that standard operating procedure.

Then monitor, measure, and document going forward. Follow up. Reward success, and don't accept failure.

MANAGEMENT CHALLENGE #15:
WHEN THERE IS CONFLICT BETWEEN AND AMONG INDIVIDUALS ON YOUR TEAM

Let's face it: Sometimes people just don't like each other. I hear from managers every day struggling to deal with interpersonal conflict between and among employees on their teams. This is one of the most common and vexing challenges managers face. Negative social dynamics at work—interpersonal conflict among coworkers—cause stress, diminish cooperation, and have a measurable impact on productivity, quality, morale, and turnover.

At the individual level, the least likeable characters in any workplace are those tackled in challenge #14—porcupines, entanglers, debaters, complainers and blamers, and stink-bomb throwers. If you can help those characters replace their negative behaviors with good communication habits, you will eliminate the most common sources of interpersonal conflict.

However, not all attitude problems in the workplace are clearly attributable to any one person, exactly. Some derive from social dynamics. Sometimes team conflict is just a clash between two particular individuals. Other times it's more complex. Sometimes everybody is implicated somehow or another.

If there is a high level of interpersonal conflict on your team, you need to ask yourself, "Why do my direct reports have enough time on their hands at work—not to mention enough brain space—to focus on interpersonal conflicts with each other?"

We've learned in our research that interpersonal conflict between and among employees is almost always an indication of undermanagement. Interpersonal conflict in the workplace has room to flower only in a relative leadership vacuum.

If you don't have clear, regularly enforced standard operating procedures, you leave room for clashes of style and preference. If you don't have good performance management in place, there will be more rivalry for attention, resources, recognition, and reward. If you are not spelling out expectations and tracking performance, employees blame each other for problems that occur and resent each other because there is no real accountability.

If you are the leader, your first step is to fill the leadership vacuum. That does not mean putting your foot down. It means getting everybody more focused on doing all that work they have in common, so they won't have as much energy to focus on conflicts. You don't need a big moment. You need a good process. Take a look at your use of team meetings and one-on-ones to make sure you are practicing the fundamentals regularly and consistently. What do you need to do to fill that leadership vacuum?

If you get back to practicing the fundamentals with discipline, you will suck the oxygen right out of most conflicts. Make sure every individual is highly focused every day on getting lots of work done very well, very fast. Remind everybody repeatedly about the broad performance standards—including the standards for good professional communication, cooperation, and mutual support.

When you are coaching employees every day, spelling out expectations, and tracking performance every step of the way, employees are less likely to worry about each other and more likely to worry about getting their own work done. And the more focused everyone is on the work they have in common, the more likely they are to cooperate. Most of the intramural conflicts will fall away under your strong, highly engaged leadership. When conflicts occur, you will know what's in character and out of character for each person, what rings true and what doesn't. You will be in a better position to evaluate and make appropriate decisions.

If you find lingering conflicts on your team, even after you've filled the leadership vacuum, chances are you are fighting a conflict that has had too much time and space to fester and grow. Perhaps it's an unresolved personality clash that has left ill will. Or maybe cliques have formed, ringleaders have emerged, or even bullies. You need to identify the problem and treat it aggressively. Beware: surgical removal of the "tumor" may be required if aggressive treatment does not swiftly render it benign.

When there is ill will between specific colleagues, you need to confront the situation directly. You cannot be the judge and jury for every argument between employees. But who else is going to adjudicate? For past "wrongs," the only question is: What can and should be done now? You are going to have to hear out both parties and then make a judgment call. That means you need to be sufficiently engaged that you can evaluate the situation. Either you make a decision that everybody needs to live with, or else the issue remains in status quo—and that, too, is a decision. In any case, everybody needs to live with the decision and agree to move on.

Going forward, you have another decision to make: Will you make an effort to keep them apart in the future, working on different projects, in different areas, or on different shifts? Or will they need to be able to work together? If it's the latter, then they need to establish a regular, ongoing, one-on-one dialogue with each other and agree on ground rules for how they are going to work together in a cooperative and professional manner.

If certain employees are especially prone to conflicts—in repeated instances—you need to aggressively coach the conflict-prone employees on avoiding conflict and to interact in more positive ways. Tell them what to say and how to say it so that they can engage in conflict-free interactions. Spell it out. Break it down. Follow up.

You rarely find cliques without ringleaders. Often cliques form around competing ringleaders. Sometimes ringleaders emerge from within a clique. But they almost always go together. The real nature of the problem with cliques and ringleaders is that they constitute a parallel power structure, chain of command, and system of communication. That creates confusion and dissent, at best. You cannot allow that to continue.

You have two choices when it comes to cliques and ringleaders: either co-opt the parallel power structure or break it up. Co-opting means turning the clique into a team and the ringleader into a deputy. You have to ask yourself: Is the ringleader demonstrating natural leadership ability and having a positive impact? Does the clique make sense as a team? If the answer to both questions is "yes," then maybe deputizing the ringleader as captain of the team-clique is a good idea. Otherwise, you need to break up the parallel power structure: remove the bad apples, reassign key players, and/or impose a strong chain of command that displaces the ringleader and disrupts the clique.

When it comes to bullying in the workplace, those are the easy cases. That is a zero-tolerance issue. If anybody in the workplace is abusive to anyone else in any way—menacing, threatening, or even suggesting violent words or actions—this is a matter of public safety. As a manager, you have a responsibility to keep everybody safe in that workplace. Any behavior like that must be removed from the workplace immediately—period.

MANAGEMENT CHALLENGE #16:
WHEN AN EMPLOYEE HAS PERSONAL ISSUES AT HOME

I said in this chapter's opening that the only way to effectively manage attitude at work is not to let it be a personal matter, but rather to make it all about the work. What about when it really is a personal matter that's causing the problem?

Surely any solution you can possibly come up with simply must be a workplace-based solution. But it's helpful to know when there is a precipitating event in the employee's life outside of work that affects the employee's state of mind at work. It might be a new thing or long-standing; long-lasting or passing; big or not so big; sudden or gradually unfolding. In some cases the personal problem is obvious; in others it may be a bit of a mystery at first.

When something is happening in an employee's life outside of work that negatively affects the employee at work, it can be very serious. For instance, it could be a clear medical issue—perhaps a newly discovered or acquired illness, or a disability of the employee himself or a close family member. In such cases, you would understand fully that it is not your job to try to be that employee's doctor. Make sure you respect that individual's rights and privacy—make any reasonable accommodations that you can for the person. Be kind and decent. Perhaps your organization has some kind of employer-sponsored resources, such as an EAP (employee assistance program), that can help the employee. You should help that employee find the right resource. Understand that the employee might have to take some time off—whatever sort of paid and unpaid leave is available for medical needs. Direct the employee to HR.

Not all issues are so straightforward. You just never know how employees are going to respond—at work or otherwise—to the things happening in their personal lives. Most people try to compartmentalize those personal challenges and keep them out of work. Some people don't or won't. Sometimes they can't.

Remember that everybody—everybody—has a personal life. Some personal lives are more challenging than others. But everybody has personal challenges. There are some personal issues that are tough for anyone—even the most private compartmentalizer—to keep under wraps. The whole range of serious and difficult personal issues that affect human beings can show up at work in an employee at any time: substance abuse, violence (domestic or otherwise), abuse (violent or otherwise), divorce, death, birth, fire, floods, depression, compulsion, among many others.

Over the years, I've seen many managers get drawn into such highly personal matters with employees. It's almost always a mistake. Don't do it. It is time-consuming and almost never works. Sometimes there are negative repercussions that are hard to shake.

Managers often ask me, "When an employee is wearing his personal pain on his sleeve at work, don't you need to acknowledge that and ask about it?" The answer: Yes, of course. The best practice in this situation is to be aware, be kind, and be brief about it.

The question you should ask yourself is, "How much do you need to know about what's going on in an employee's personal life?" The answer: you probably want to know enough to be polite. What you need to know is how an employee's personal life bears on his role at work.

It is not your job to be any employee's therapist. You are not qualified, and it's not appropriate. Nor should you try to be any employee's life coach or counselor. You should not, nor do you need to, be trying to help this person manage or solve his or her problems at home. You need to help this person manage and solve his or her problems at work.

It's clarifying to reframe this very complicated issue in clear and simple terms: "Is this person having troubles at work?" No matter what the problem is outside of work, what you need to do is make it completely clear that what's going on at work is 100 percent the work. That's not just hard-nosed boss talk. That can also be a real kindness.

Acknowledge that something may be going on outside of work. Ask if the employee wants to share with you the nature of the issue. Stop and evaluate whether or not your knowledge of that personal issue now obligates you to take action at work. Does the issue pose a danger to anyone at work? Evaluate whether this person is going to need some time off, and/or whether there are employee assistance resources that might help this person. If not, then the biggest favor you can do for this person and yourself and the rest of the team at work is refocus the discussion on the work: "Here are the performance standards. And here are the concrete expectations. Your time at work is measured entirely by meeting and exceeding those performance standards and concrete expectations. Exceed those standards and expectations, and no matter how bad you might be feeling outside of work, you can feel great about your time here."

Of course, if an employee simply cannot leave those personal issues outside of work—if the employee cannot at least meet the standards and expectations at work—then the employee might need some time off or a leave of absence, or to be removed from the job entirely. You should always make every effort to help this employee avail himself of any employee assistance resources you possibly can. You could even volunteer to help personally somehow, outside of work. You can and should be very kind. But you just can't have that person at work if he or she is not able to perform at work.

Maybe you are thinking, "Ah, but these are the very special cases." Indeed. But remember, every employee is a special case. Some are just much better at hiding that fact at work than others. Keep your eyes and ears open for the signs and symptoms of personal issues outside of work, but keep your ongoing dialogue focused on the work.

When addressing personal issues with an employee:

- Acknowledge that something may be going on outside of work and ask if the employee wants to share with you the nature of the issue.
- Do not try to help employees manage or solve their problems at home.
- Make it 100 percent clear that what's going on at work is 100 percent the work.
- Evaluate: Does the issue pose a danger to anyone at work? Does this person need time off or time away? Are there employee assistance resources that might help this person?
- Refocus the ongoing discussion on the work: performance standards and concrete expectations.

CHAPTER SIX

The Challenges of Managing Superstars

Let's cut right to the chase: the very best talent—at every level—is worth so much more than other employees that the only way to be fair, keep them motivated, retain them, and develop them is to differentiate radically and invest wildly in recognizing and rewarding them.

You know very well that one truly great player on your team is worth three, four, or five mediocre people. The difference in value is sometimes hard to quantify, sometimes not so hard. Think about that MVP, that superstar, that employee you can rely on without hesitation. The one who (almost) always gets the job done right and ahead of schedule, takes exactly the right amount of initiative without overstepping, makes good decisions on tough judgment calls, and does it all with a big smile on her face. Day after day, the superstar proves her disproportionate value: bringing her best to work, continuously learning and growing, going the extra mile, contributing great ideas, and influencing others with her commitment and enthusiasm.

What would you do to hire that superstar? Just think of the value she could add. You would probably commit to:

- Investing more time and attention in coaching and developing
- Paying generously, especially in bonuses for going above and beyond
- Flexible work arrangements

If you wouldn't, what are you thinking?

What would you do if you lost your most valuable player, today? The answer: suffer. Plenty. Among the very worst days of your career are the ones when one of your superstars comes to tell you, "Thanks for everything. I'm going to be leaving for a new opportunity." Imagine (or remember), this is somebody you really value, somebody you've invested in for weeks, months, or years. And that person tells you she's going to be walking out the door with your investment.

It can be so costly in money, time, effort, and morale. Everybody has to scramble to fill in the gaps. No matter how much everybody scrambles, details slip through the cracks. That superstar was juggling so many balls, some of them are bound to drop. You have to get somebody new, fast, and then you're going to have to get that new person up to speed before the rest of the team (and you) can start making up for the time you've lost. More than likely, you'll end up going through a time-consuming (and expensive) hiring process to replace the person you've lost. And the more old-fashioned the organization, the more involved the hiring process will be. When a replacement is finally chosen, it will take too long to get her on board and up to speed so she can start adding value.

What are you doing right now to make sure that doesn't happen to you? What are you doing to keep your superstars highly engaged, connected, committed, and happy to stay? How do you get the superstars to stay for the long term?

It used to be that you could pretty well count on the best people you recruited to rise to the top, while the mediocre people would drop off along the way. You didn't expect everybody who came to work for you to achieve a long-term successful career in your organization. There was a challenge hanging out there in front of people when they walked in your door: "Can you make it here?" The best people would rise to that challenge. Nowadays, it seems the best people are often the most likely to leave. Why? Because they are the ones who can. In today's transactional employment market, they are in danger of leaving long before they've paid their dues—or even paid a return on your recruiting and training investment.

Access to the best talent has always been critical to the success of any enterprise. That's nothing new. But if today's lean, flexible organizations are going to succeed, they need to get more work and better work out of fewer people. That means those few people have to be very, very good.

That's why, regardless of fluctuations in the labor market, there is likely to be a growing premium on people, at all ends of the skill spectrum, who can work smarter, faster, and better. You want your people to be innovative (within guidelines), passionate (within reason), and armed with sufficient discretion to make mistakes (as long as they are not too big). Demand for those people is going to outpace supply for the foreseeable future. Technology will continue to improve, organizations will become even leaner, the pace of change will get even faster, competition will be even more intense, businesses will become even more customer focused, expected response times will get shorter, and productivity expectations will grow.

That superstar is the senior executive talent who can turn around a division in eighteen months. That superstar is the programmer who can write two lines of code for every one that an ordinary programmer writes. And that superstar is the call-center operator who can dazzle every customer, gather market research on the front lines, and routinely suggest improvements in the whole system. And the salesperson in the field who can sell anything to anybody and who also monitors warehouse inventory and the production schedule from his handheld device. And the warehouse manager everybody knows by name, the one who also knows the new database inside and out. That superstar is the factory worker who doubles as a quality control engineer. He's the nonphysician health professional delivering care previously obtainable only from doctors.

The superstar is very valuable, and she knows it. She is always going to gravitate to managers who recognize and reward her value and are prepared to invest in building her up and making her even more valuable.

Too often managers lose superstars (or fail to hire them in the first place) due to a lack of discretion and/or resources necessary to properly recognize and reward them. But just as often it's simply a lack of imagination.

An advertising executive once told me about what he called a "career-altering mistake in talent management." He had a superstar employee in a critical position who came to him and announced she needed to work, for the foreseeable future, only three days a week in the office. She wanted to work at home on Thursdays and not at all on Fridays. The ad exec says:

> She had fantastic people skills, was super-creative, could dazzle clients, and had great experience both in spearheading focused product research, interpreting it, and spinning it into a great creative message. She also had great experience with both multi-media campaigns. She had the strength of personality to handle accounts from the pitching new business stage, all the way through the final execution of a high-level multimedia adver-tising campaign. She was one of a kind. But three days a week and one from home? It just didn't seem like we could do that. It would have made her an "elite" employee with a sweetheart deal. We were worried how other employees would react. I made my expectations very clear, that I didn't think it was a part-time job. And she said she didn't want a part-time job, either. She expected a full-time position, with full-time pay, full-time position benefits and administrative support, and she expected to be on the fast track to partnership. But she wanted to work at home on Thursdays and not at all on Fridays.

I asked, "What did you really think?"

He said, "In all honesty, I knew darned well she could do a lot more in four days a week than most very good people would do in five, but we just couldn't go there. So we let her leave. And I paid for it for a long time."

This woman was phenomenally valuable, and she knew it. She believed she could demand whatever she wanted, or she wouldn't have been so demanding. If she had been able to arrange the terms she needed, do you think her performance would have declined or improved? Do you think she would leave the company that arranged those conditions for her any time soon? Not likely. The ad exec said, "If I had the chance all over again, I'd make her an elite employee with a sweetheart deal in a heartbeat."

You want a whole team of superstars. But if you've got one, I'll bet the last thing in the world you want is to lose her. Whether or not your superstars are currently driving a hard bargain, you want to pay them what you know they are worth—in both financial and nonfinancial rewards:

- **Invest in your superstars in every way you possibly can.** That means your time and every training, development, and stretch-assignment opportunities you can muster, not to mention the best resources of every sort.
- **Pay the superstars what they are worth**—especially when they go the extra mile—even if it is more than you pay their counterparts who produce less.
- **Be flexible about where or when those superstars work**, in most cases, as long as they get the job done very well and ahead of schedule.

In a free market, you get what you can negotiate. As the manager, you do have the discretion and resources to differentiate those superstars in the way they deserve to be recognized and rewarded. If every condition of employment—not just pay, but schedule, duration of employment, location, assignments, and so on—is on the table, your negotiating position as a manager is stronger, not weaker.

After all, you are a manager:

- You decide which employees to give the most one-on-one time and how much you prepare for that time with each employee.
- You assign the choice projects (and the really horrendous ones).
- You make the schedule.

- You decide who is going to work with whom.
- You may have the power to relocate people from one city to another, or even from one country to another, or at least from work station to work station.
- You have a substantial influence on your employees' paychecks and on their prospects for promotion.
- You do their performance reviews.
- You even have some discretionary resources to dole out—office space, training opportunities, exposure to decision makers, time off, maybe even cash.

Providing more generous rewards and work conditions to reward and retain high performers is a workplace trend that is not going to reverse for the foreseeable future, regardless of fluctuations in the labor market. Business leaders understand it because it dovetails with the strong trends toward employee ranking and pay for performance.

In our research, we've learned that providing differential recognition and rewards works only when managers do the hard work of shining that bright light of scrutiny on every employee. Start by shining the brightest light on the superstars. They deserve it. That's also how you make it clear to everybody that the superstars are in fact doing more, faster, and better with the best attitude, and they are being rewarded for it. They are setting the high standard—the examples to be followed by ambitious employees who aspire to be superstars too.

That may sound reasonable in theory, but most managers believe they have painfully insufficient time, discretion, and resources available to truly differentiate high performers. Rather than devoting the lion's share of their time and attention to superstars, managers are often thankful that they don't have to worry about the superstars' work, that they don't need hand-holding. When a superstar actually knocks on the manager's door and says he wants to work just three days a week on site and from home on Thursdays, the manager might look that superstar in the eye and explain: "I can't let employees choose their own schedules, even superstars. That would be granting special privileges to one employee." The manager might say, "That wouldn't seem fair."

On the other hand, the manager doesn't want to lose the superstar or make him unhappy or be at odds with him. So maybe the manager gives in to his request. But the classic mistake that so many managers make in this situation is that they make the secret deal: "OK, *superstar. I'll make that secret deal with you. But don't tell anybody.*" Pretty soon, the manager has "average" performers knocking on the door saying, "I understand superstar made his own schedule, three days on site, Thursdays from home. That's not fair! You are playing favorites. I'd like to make my own schedule too."

How do you explain to the average employees that you are indeed playing favorites, very much on purpose?! You are favoring superstars because they do more work, better, faster, with a better attitude. They are more valuable. You want to explain to the average employees: "The superstars do more work. They get here early and stay late. They take exactly the right amount of initiative without overstepping." You want to challenge the average employees: "Let's start talking in our regular one-on-ones about how you too can someday be a superstar. Let's start talking about how you can begin moving down the path to higher performance so you can earn more! Let's start talking about how you can do more work, faster, and better, and maybe even with a better attitude. Let's start talking about how we can start putting you in a position to earn more recognition and rewards. One step at a time, one day at a time." What do you think would happen if you had the discretion, the ability, the skill, and the gumption to start negotiating with employees as if every single reward and detriment were tied solely to measurable instances of employee performance?

Every employee worth employing—and for sure any superstar— wants to know what they need to do to earn more in each of these areas. Help people by telling them exactly what they need to do to earn more. You have to be very clear with your employees and remind them on a regular basis: "OK. Here's the deal. For coming in to work on time, for not leaving early, and for getting a lot of work done very well without causing any problems, you get paid. And you get to keep working here!" Those are the fundamentals of the employment deal. Your employees should understand that doing their jobs very well, very fast, all day long is what they were hired to do. That's why they get paid a basic wage or salary with benefits.

Beyond the basic requirements of the job, employees should know that if they need or want more, they have to earn those rewards through their own hard work. As part of your regular, ongoing one-on-one dialogues with everybody, every step of the way:

- Give every person the chance to meet the basic expectations of his or her job and then the chance to go above and beyond—and to be rewarded accordingly.

- Look at the discretionary resources that are at your disposal already. Use your precious one-on-one time; your power over work conditions, scheduling, and recognition; your access to decision makers; your leeway to decide what tasks are assigned to whom, who gets extra training opportunities, where each employee works, and with what coworker; and so on.

- Do whatever you can to extend your discretionary resources and look for every opportunity to use those resources to drive and reward exceptional performance, across the board, but especially with the superstars.

- Create trust and confidence through open communication and transparency so that every employee knows exactly what she has to do to earn rewards—no matter how great or small those rewards might be.

- Monitor, measure, and document it every step of the way.

- Don't flinch when it comes to providing the promised rewards and detriments that people earn through their choices and behavior.

Of course, you can't do everything for everybody. And why would you ever want to?

Make clear who you are rewarding, how, and why. Maybe others will work hard to earn special rewards, too. That's why it's so important to make sure every employee knows how and why she is earning her rewards and what she needs to do in order to earn more (or to be allowed to earn less in exchange for more flexibility).

How do you do that? By defining expectations and tying concrete rewards directly to the fulfillment of those expectations. When every person on your team is managed this way, they are much less likely to wonder why another person is receiving special rewards. Every single one of them knows from experience what they have to do to earn special rewards. They know that if a superstar is receiving some special attention, recognition, or reward from you, he must have earned it. After all, that's the kind of manager you are.

Whatever you are doing to be flexible and generous to retain your good employees, you need to be much more flexible and generous to keep your great employees engaged, motivated, and committed. When favoring superstars, consider these guidelines:

• Whatever one-on-one time you give to your good employees, spend more time with your superstars and prepare for that time like you are preparing for a meeting with your boss's boss. Make sure your one-on-ones with superstars are a great use of everybody's time.

• However your good employees are assigned to work with vendors, customers, coworkers, subordinates, and managers, give your great employees first choice in relationship opportunities at work.

• However tasks and responsibilities are assigned to good employees, give your great employees first choice. Give the great ones first choice on any special projects or choice assignments.

• Whatever training opportunities are being made available to good employees, offer the best training resources to the best people first.

• Whatever you are you paying your good employees, pay your great ones more. Consider giving them more in base pay and benefits.

Definitely give them more bonus money contingent on clear performance benchmarks tied directly to concrete actions they can control.

• Whatever kind of scheduling flexibility you are providing for your good employees, give your great ones the best schedules, and give them more control over when they work.

• However good employees are assigned to work locations or work spaces and travel, give the best people the first choice of location, work space, and travel.

The more you can help the superstars customize their roles, work conditions, and ability to get paid, the longer you will keep them engaged, motivated, and committed. You can be sure that the superstar is thrilled at the prospect of building the next stage of her career. The only questions are: Will the superstar be thrilled to do that on *this* team, reporting to you? And do you have what it takes to continue leading this superstar?

MANAGEMENT CHALLENGE #17:
WHEN THERE IS A SUPERSTAR YOU
NEED TO KEEP ENGAGED

If you are in charge of a superstar, then *you* must be a super superstar. Right? That's a lot of pressure. One of the awkward secrets of managing superstars is that many managers are not 100 percent sure they really have what it takes to continue leading that superstar.

Sometimes managers fool themselves into thinking that their superstars are so talented, skilled, and motivated that they don't need to be managed at all. But even superstars need to be managed. Just like everyone else, superstars have bad days and lapses in judgment, and sometimes they go in the wrong direction. Even superstars need guidance, direction, support, and encouragement. Most of all, superstars want to be challenged and developed.

Sometimes managers tell me, "This superstar is different. She is so talented, skilled, and motivated that I have nothing to offer her." If that's truly the case, it doesn't mean the person doesn't need a manager. It just means you are second-guessing whether you are up to the challenge. You don't need to be an Olympic athlete to be a great coach. You need to be, first and foremost, reliably persistent, consistently engaged, providing that regular touchpoint of accountability—at the very least, a mirror always there to provide an honest source of feedback. The superstar wants a performance coach who knows exactly what she is doing; one who is in a position to help her do more, faster, and better, and to keep track of her successes.

Too often, here's what happens instead: Managers let themselves off the hook, thusly: "Does this superstar really need me? I've got other, more pressing things to deal with. I'm just glad to have someone I don't have to worry about." The manager then inadvertently neglects that superstar for days or weeks or months at a time. Why would you ever do that? Because you know that the building isn't going to burn down if you leave the superstar alone. You know she can handle everything that is thrown at her and more. In fact, you lean on her plenty as your unofficial backup on everything. You expect the most from her. You demand the most from her, or at least request the most, knowing darned well that she rarely says "no." Rather than lavishing the superstar with attention and privileges, you heap new responsibilities on her already formidable pile, often without giving her guidance and direction because you know she is so good she'll figure it out on her own. The superstar is self-starting and highly motivated. She doesn't need you to pat her on the back every day. She's so good, she must know that you appreciate her value. At least you *hope* she knows that you will find a way to recognize and reward her properly for her contribution soon—just not now, please.

Here's the problem: As soon as you start neglecting the superstar, you cease to be that special performance coach who will be a central player in building this next stage in her career progression. Why would you give up that role? Yet we see this in our research all the time. Superstars want to fill that role in their careers. If you give up that role, they will fill it with someone else before long. As soon as you give up that role, you start to lose the superstar.

Case in point:

"We are repeatedly surprised, but we shouldn't be anymore, when we see which of the [professionals] stay and which ones leave, especially in recent years," I was told by a senior executive in a large financial services firm. The finance exec continued: "Of course, we know who the very high-potential employees are and who are the highest performing. I used to be able to predict which ones would stay. But in recent years, I have been repeatedly surprised. It seems the ones who have the most get-up-and-go are no longer the most likely to stay. They are the most likely to get up and go."

When we looked into the matter, here's what we found: The culture of the firm was such that employees who were doing the best job were least likely to have contact with their senior managers. The senior managers were spending way too much time on a few low performers, and nowhere near enough time with the high performers. The superstar who was a fast learner—who immediately gets with the program, stays busy, and solves his own problems as they come up—was the very least likely to interact with his manager. Very quickly the superstars felt that they didn't have a mentor or coach or teacher to help them learn and grow, and they started to look elsewhere. They were elite performers, and as such they wanted to work with highly engaged coaching-style leaders. When I shared this finding with the finance exec and his colleagues, they were no longer surprised: "You don't worry about those high performers for the very reason that they are high performers, and then the next day that person is leaving. We need to turn this around."

The solution was simple: we turned it around by turning that culture on its head. Superstars should not get the least time and attention from senior leaders; rather, they should get the most. The better the superstar, the more time and attention they get. Simple as that!

Here's where it got complicated: Many of the senior managers wanted some guidance:

What do we talk about with the superstar? After all, this person is so talented, skilled, and motivated that she is able to handle more responsibility than most. She can make her own project plans; she gets lots of work done very well, very fast, all day, every day; she doesn't cause problems; she learns quickly and steadily; she has great relationship skills; she understands the big picture; she is a great critical thinker; and she takes exactly the right amount of initiative without overstepping. She's so on top of things: She wants to get out there and sell! I don't want to waste the superstar's time. How do I make sure the one-on-ones are a good use of time?

One senior manager offered: "It really requires me to take the one-on-ones to the next level. It puts a lot of pressure on me. I have to bring more to the table. I prepare in advance, and we engage in a much higher-level conversation as a result of that. This way, I'm able to keep challenging those really high performers and helping them continue to challenge themselves. And I'm learning a lot from the process myself." Indeed, you can learn so much from coaching superstars.

Instead of neglecting your regular one-on-ones with your superstars, double down on them. Put your one-on-ones with superstars at the top of your priority list, ahead of one-on-ones with the low performers. Then take those one-on-ones with your superstars to the next level. To keep a superstar engaged:

- Prepare more, not less, for every one-on-one.

- Always check regularly to make sure that things are going as well as you think. Just like everybody else, superstars need to provide regular reports on their tasks, responsibilities, and projects. Regardless of their talents, you need to verify that the work is getting done.

- Pay close attention to how superstars challenge you in ways that you don't expect. Learn from the way they force you to stay on your toes and think on your feet.

- Brainstorm about recurring problems and innovative solutions.

- Learn from their frontline intelligence ("What's really going on out there?"). And learn from their analysis ("What do *you* make of what's going on out there?").

- Help them pursue technical expertise, professional training, and any specialized knowledge.

- Make sure they get their needs met and aren't looking for another job. Go out of your way regularly to ask, "What do you need from me?" Keep track of their great work, and look for ways to provide them with special rewards.

- Challenge superstars to be peer leaders and to take ad hoc leadership opportunities like short-term projects and teams. And coach them every step of the way.

- Teach them the tricks and the shortcuts, warn them of pitfalls, and help them solve problems. Support them through bad days and counsel them through difficult judgment calls.

- Once in a while, talk strategically about how superstars should navigate their careers within the organization. Discuss how work assignments have been going and what assignments should be sought next; new training opportunities, transfers to new work groups, or moves to new locations. You might recommend strategies for pursuing raises, promotions, or desired work conditions. The idea is to offer regular career advice from an insider's perspective so they don't have to get it from outsiders (like from headhunters).

- Use your influence and authority in the organization to make sure that the most valuable players are getting the lion's share of resources to support and accelerate their career success. Talk regularly with your superstars to make certain that nothing has gone or is going wrong in their work assignments. Steer them to the best training opportunities, the choice projects and assignments, and the most powerful decision makers. Fast-track them to win bonuses, raises, promotions, and desired work conditions.

WHEN YOU HAVE A SUPERSTAR YOU
REALLY WANT TO RETAIN

For many years we have advised organizations of all shapes and sizes on best practices for employee retention and how to control employee turnover. Sometimes senior executives will call me in a panic over one particular superstar whom the executive is suddenly afraid might leave: "He has one foot out the door. What can we possibly do to keep him?"

One of my favorite calls of all time was from exactly the other end of the spectrum: "Great news: She did have one foot out the door after all, but now I'm quite certain she's not going anywhere ever!" That call came from a senior executive in a huge multinational company in the mining industry (I'll call him "Gold").

I knew that Gold had been very worried about losing a very promising protégé with whom he had been working closely, mentoring and developing for nearly two years (I'll call the protégé "Silver"). There was no question Silver was a superstar and she was going places. She had a Ph.D. in geophysical engineering and an MBA. She carried U.S. and EU citizenship, spoke multiple languages, and had life experiences that had seasoned her. Gold had invested a huge amount of time as well as significant resources in Silver's growth and development. Gold had brought Silver into high-level meetings, exposed her to powerful decision makers, and included her in the details of complex transactions. He was cultivating a deputy and, perhaps ten years down the road, a successor in his role. Gold had said many times: "I'm telling you—Silver could be the CEO of this entire company." By the way, she was only thirty-three.

Needless to say, Silver was courted in grand fashion by many other potential employers. She got calls from headhunters every day, not to mention senior executives and even CEOs of other companies in or around the mining industry. Silver was one of those people who could write her own ticket, name her own terms. Gold could see that his considerable development investment in Silver was at risk. Gold had already leveraged every last budget dollar to pay her a high salary, but any other employer could just match that money and eliminate that as a factor. Money alone was not going to solve the problem. The solution would have to come from a more interesting currency, something less easy to match in dollars in a bidding contest. The key would be to identify the nonfinancial factors that were really important to Silver and find a way to create a customized work situation that would be very hard to replicate at another employer.

My advice to Gold: "Find out what Silver's ideal work conditions would be—other than money. Tell her to design her dream job." Nobody quits a dream job.

Here's what Silver wanted: She wanted to be based in the San Francisco Bay Area (although Gold and his team were based in Salt Lake City, Utah). She wanted to work directly with Gold and only on his deals. She wanted to work thirty-eight weeks a year, according to a strict calendar of weeks on and fourteen weeks off. (She agreed she could be available for a limited number of meetings during her weeks off.) She wanted her travel time limited to 50 percent of her schedule. She wanted to be paid at 100 percent full-time with full access to all benefits, bonuses, promotions, and raises. She wanted a full-time staff assistant based in the Bay Area with her and dedicated 100 percent to supporting her. There was more, but that was the gist of it.

Gold gave her everything she wanted. And he was right. She was not going anywhere. Nobody quits a dream job.

Sometimes business leaders become incensed when I tell them this story: "It's like being held up for blackmail: 'Give me a dream job or I'll quit and take your training and development investment with me to your competition!' We can't negotiate with terrorists!"

Here's my response: Why shouldn't employees who are worth more negotiate for the best deal they can possibly get? Are you a communist? The imperative of negotiating generous terms and conditions with the best talent is just the application of free market principles to employment relationships. Employment is a transactional relationship.

The question is: Will you have the imagination to negotiate fair and compelling deals with your superstars? And will you be able to muster the discretion and resources to make those deals? The best people at every level should be in a position to negotiate the best deals. When a valuable person goes to the trouble of customizing his work situation— negotiating special arrangements with the organization, his manager, and his coworkers—his stake in the position grows tremendously. His investment in the organization, his commitment, his willingness to deliver results grows.

Money is, by its nature, interchangeable. Custom work conditions most certainly are not. If money is the primary currency you have for negotiating with talent, it is very easy for your employees to measure it against deals offered by other employers. Just so you know: other employers tend to pay people in money too. More is always better. Any substantial differential in financial opportunity is hard to resist.

Make your value very difficult for the employee to match anywhere else. Based on our research, these are the five nonfinancial factors of an employment relationship that people care the most about:

1. When they work (schedule)
2. Where they work (location)
3. What they do (tasks and responsibilities)
4. Who they work with
5. What they are (or are not) learning on the job

If you let people customize these factors, they will design their dream job. The dream job factors are the most valuable currency you can possibly offer as an employer.

Sometimes managers push back at this point: "Well, if I had all the flexibility in the world (not to mention the resources) then, sure, I could retain just about anybody too." But of course not all work is amenable to every customization. Retail stores, for example, must be open certain hours on certain days. A grocery store cashier can't very well work from home. A factory worker must be at the plant in order to use the assembly equipment.

You need to start by focusing on the work that needs to be done. Examine every task and responsibility. Then ask yourself: Does this need to be done in a particular building during certain hours? Sometimes the answer is yes—both time and place are nonnegotiable elements of the work. However, often time or place or both are negotiable. Then there is room to customize—all that is left to do is negotiate the terms.

When managers set about this process, they almost always find that when examining a particular role, some tasks and responsibilities in a person's job are flexible—especially as to time and place—while others are not. The job, therefore, looks as if it cannot be customized. So it is necessary to unbundle the package of tasks and responsibilities that currently make up the job, rearrange the elements, and make a new package—a more flexible role. If a person is willing to continue working for you, for example, but only from home, you may have to adjust that person's role so that it consists of only tasks that can be done from home.

It is rarely necessary to customize 100 percent of every dimension that may or may not matter to the employee. Almost always, a particular individual has one or two dream job factors that really matter to him. Perhaps he has a child. What if the child is sick Tuesday morning and neither parent's work schedule is free? Inevitably, work must come second for at least one parent that Tuesday morning. This sort of thing happens every day at any workplace. The only question is: Has the parent negotiated enough scheduling flexibility that the parenting doesn't compromise his success at work? Many people have just one or two scheduling issues that really get in their way. A small adjustment can have a tremendous impact. Sometimes the customization a person wants has to do with the work she is doing: one person hates database work, whereas another loves it. The right match between a person's interests and her work can make the difference between a job that is "just a job" and one that is worthy of her very best efforts.

No doubt some of your employees will have needs that cannot be met: George loves the company, but he is dying to work in Paris. You don't have a Paris office. You are not going to be able to customize the job to his satisfaction. It's OK. You can't please everybody all the time. But so often there *are* things you can do that really matter to people if you are willing to make small accommodations. To the person who really cares, the value of those small accommodations will be immeasurable.

Should people have to earn the custom features of their jobs? Of course. And they should keep earning them. Negotiate whatever terms make sense. When you make a deal, both sides are expected to deliver. And the deal is always open, changing over time as the organization's needs change and the person's availability and circumstances change.

I should add this warning: sometimes performance problems will occur as you negotiate custom work situations. That's because people can be wrong in their self-evaluations, just as employers can be wrong in their assumptions. An employee's insistent "I really want to work from home" can turn into a plaintive "I can't concentrate at home. I just end up not getting my work done." That doesn't have to mean the whole deal is off; it just means the deal needs to be renegotiated. If the source of the performance problem is obvious (for example, since the person started working from home, his productivity has diminished substantially), then a smart manager will cut short the arrangement and renegotiate, making a deal that eliminates the problem-causing factors.

But that rarely happens, especially with superstars. People are usually so thrilled to customize their work arrangements that they become very protective of the deal they've created for themselves. In a results-based relationship, where engagement and accountability are high, that self-protection almost always manifests in exceptional performance. Often people perform much better when they have flexible work arrangements because they don't want any question to arise that might compromise their situation. When people work out their custom deals, they will work doubly hard to prove themselves and keep the deal in place. And they won't be going to work anywhere else any time soon.

What about when the manager has limited discretion and limited resources with which to retain her most valuable employees? Often managers tell me they struggle with this. One general manager of a supermarket in a large chain said: "I don't have million-dollar employees. But I still have employees who are super valuable to me. My produce manager. My deli manager. If I lose them, I'm in trouble. What can I do in a nickel-and-dime game to retain those kinds of superstars?"

Indeed, with fewer resources and less discretion, it's a whole lot harder. Concentrate on finding opportunities to favor your superstars every step of the way. Not only that, but make it clear who you are favoring, why, and exactly what it would take for others to get the same favorable treatment.

Here's the plan that supermarket GM got approved at corporate and rolled out as a pilot in his store. He worked with each of his top department managers—his superstars—on reallocating their labor budgets. They took the total available amount of money and thought about how to free up money for additional compensation for themselves and their teams. These are not the highest-paying jobs, so every little bit helps. That's what was at stake for these individuals. In each case, faced with that option, the superstar manager cut the equivalent of one-and-a-half full-time employees (sixty hours a week) from the team and then split up the money between himself (the manager) and his remaining team members, in the form of overtime pay. So the remaining team members all worked more, but the additional hours were paid at time-and-a-half because they were hourly. In each case, the team members cut were the weakest employees and those who remained were stronger. Without the weaker members, there were fewer problems to solve, fewer messes to clean up. And no more people just not showing up for their shifts. Among the remaining team members there was greater cohesion and support for each other. They all had to work more hours now, which put pressure on their nonwork lives. But they were also much more understanding of each other and more willing to cover for each other when necessary. Plus they were all very glad to be taking home a significant amount of additional money.

With this plan, this supermarket GM reduced turnover in the pilot departments to a fraction of what it had been and retained all four of the superstar department managers, all of whom went on to be GMs of their own stores in the chain. That was a huge win for everybody.

Don't wait for your superstars to start thinking about leaving before you start asking, "What can we do to keep you?" Start asking on their very first day of employment, and keep asking. Does that mean you should do everything for everybody? No. Why would you want to?

In your regular, ongoing one-on-one dialogue with every person, you should be talking about not only what you need from each person, but also about what each person needs from you. Your direct reports need to know that you understand what they want and need, that you care, and that you are going to work with them on an ongoing basis to help them earn more of it. The key is not to give them false hope or make false promises. When employees express needs and wants that are totally unrealistic, let them know that immediately so they can manage their expectations. Help them see what is realistic.

Sometimes what they want is downright easy for you to deliver. But first you have to know what they need and want. Small one-time accommodations, such as leaving early to be with a sick family member, are easy to grant and usually a matter of kindness. Failure to grant these usually costs much more than granting them. But of course, you can't let employees take advantage. If an employee wants to leave early every afternoon to visit a sister in the hospital, then that's not a one-time accommodation. That's a special schedule. You can't do everything for everybody. The question is only: how much can you do for this person at this time?

Start talking with all of your direct reports about retention on day one, and keep talking about it. Zero in on the superstars early and often. If you are talking with them on an ongoing basis about how to meet their needs and wants, they are much more likely to talk with you at those key points when they are trying to decide whether to leave or stay. If you are willing to work with them, you can be flexible and generous. That's how you make them want to stay and work harder, at least for a little while longer. Those employees who turn out to be long-term employees will be the ones who decided repeatedly that they wanted to stay.

MANAGEMENT CHALLENGE #19:
WHEN YOU HAVE A SUPERSTAR YOU ARE GOING TO LOSE FOR SURE: HOW TO LOSE THAT SUPERSTAR VERY WELL

What do you do when you have a superstar who is definitely going to leave? You are past the point of any chance of retaining this person. What do you do?

Reasonable minds can differ on this question. I cannot tell you how many smart leaders and managers I know who place such a high value on loyalty that they have a very hard time forgiving someone who leaves. One finance industry CEO told me: "This is a fiercely competitive field. You are with us or you are against us. When you leave, you are taking with you your ability, skill, wisdom, institutional memory, inside knowledge, and relationships, and you are going to use those very likely to try to take food off my table. You'd better believe, you are burning your bridges when you walk away from me and this firm. Good riddance. You just became 'them.'"

In my view, that is a very limited way of looking at employment relationships, and I advise against taking that emotional and self-defeating (albeit understandable) approach if you possibly can.

The more you and your organization have invested in this employee, the more you have at stake in retaining that person—even if that person leaves, you have a huge investment to protect, no matter where he goes. Why not make sure the employee has as big a stake as possible in maintaining a good relationship with you too? You may not be able to keep the employee as a full-time, onsite, uninterrupted, exclusive employee. If you can't keep the whole employee, why not keep as much as you can? Instead of losing them, offer your most valued employees the chance to take an unpaid sabbatical or to work part-time, flextime, or as telecommuters or consultants. When your superstars leave, instead of burning the bridge, stay in close touch with them and stay on good terms. Try rerecruiting them after they've had a chance to rest or after they've had a chance to see that the grass isn't that much greener on the other side. This is all about continuing to get a return on your investment in this superstar even after the superstar has decided not to continue as an employee.

Here's the other part of the equation: If your employees know that as soon as someone mentions maybe, possibly leaving, it is tantamount to burning bridges with you, then guess what? Your employees are never going to tell you when they are thinking about leaving. They are never going to talk to you about it before it's too late. How you deal with people when they actually leave will have a huge impact on when and how employees will discuss it with you. If employees know that openly acknowledging they are thinking about leaving always means "Good riddance," then you won't know an employee is thinking about leaving until it's too late. The irony is that the only way to create an environment where employees will tell you when they are thinking about leaving is if leaving means, "Good luck to you! We'll help you in every way we can, and then let's figure out how we can maintain a great relationship going forward."

Assuming that this is a superstar you are losing, you want the goodbye to be as long as you can possibly make it. Of course, some employees, once they decide to leave, feel it's best to make it a quick and clean break. But for the superstar with whom you want to remain on very good terms going forward, make it a long goodbye to facilitate a good succession plan, comprehensive knowledge transfer, and a smooth transition.

I always remember what a senior partner in one of the big accounting consulting firms once told me: "We take succession planning very seriously—every time we lose a key person and realize there is no one on the bench ready to step in." Every superstar should be training and developing her replacement, systematically, on an ongoing basis. That should be something you talk about with your superstars in your one-on-ones with them, and your superstars talk about in their one-on-ones with their people. If your superstars don't have their own direct reports, then it's all on you. What is your succession plan for every one of your superstars? Who is on the bench being developed to step in when that superstar steps out?

Whether or not you have a person on the bench ready to step in by the time you know your superstar is leaving, you want as much time as possible so that the superstar can help train and develop her replacement. If you have the luxury to hire the replacement before the superstar is gone, you should meet with them together on a regular ongoing basis in addition to meeting with each of them separately. In other words, triple your one-on-ones for the duration of the transition period:

- Meet one-on-one with the departing superstar.
- Meet one-on-one with the new replacement player.
- Meet with the two of them together.

In your one-on-ones, focus on the intensive knowledge transfer process, from the departing superstar to the new replacement player, that should be under way. Ensure that the transfer is more than a brain-to-brain transfer, however. Every step of the way, make absolutely certain that the knowledge transfer is being documented in detail in a set of tangible information assets that can be used thereafter as learning or training tools. Ideally, these tangible knowledge transfer assets would be in the form of completely indexed and searchable, thoroughly annotated, step-by-step instructions (along with answers to frequently asked questions) for every task, responsibility, and project. The importance of creating knowledge transfer assets is even greater when you do not have the opportunity for brain-to-brain transfer; say, when there is insufficient overlapping employment of your departing superstar and his replacement.

I have to stop and note that making sure this knowledge transfer asset is built is much easier said than done. I've seen how, over and over again, despite the best intentions on everybody's part, the knowledge transfer assets built by departing superstars end up being painfully suboptimal unless the manager makes darned sure otherwise. Once you know the superstar is leaving, you need to use your one-on-ones to keep him focused on the knowledge transfer process. Make it the departing superstar's last great mission and legacy: The Superstar Memorial Annotated Standard Operating Procedures. In your one-on-ones, review the knowledge transfer document in draft form. Every step of the way, track the departing superstar's progress. Look at every set of step-by-step instructions and make sure they are clear and complete. Ask for second drafts and third drafts when necessary. If you need to, interview the departing superstar about every step in every set of SOPs to get that next level of detail.

In addition to making good use of the long goodbye, among the other best reasons to make certain that your departing superstars leave on the best possible terms is that they are likely to be valuable players wherever they go next and throughout the rest of their careers. If this person is a superstar working for you, why wouldn't she be a superstar wherever she goes? Why wouldn't you want to be on really good terms with her? Who knows—maybe she might become your valued customer in her next career? Or a valued vendor? Maybe she will come back someday and be a valued employee once again, having gained the training and development resources of another employer in the meantime?

Years ago, I was making this argument as emphatically as I knew how with the leaders of one of the top professional services firms in the world. They had asked me to come in and help them prepare for a planned long-range strategic planning meeting of the senior partners. How could they stem the tide of good people flowing out of the firm? My advice: "Let your best people work wherever they want, whenever they want, however they want. Just negotiate on an ongoing basis a market-based deal that makes sense. Buy their results on a short-term basis, on whatever terms you and they can negotiate. Don't be locked into one rigid way of employing people."

When they assured me they already offered alternative career paths, I urged them to think about their best people. "It is your best people who want the fast-track to authority and compensation, but they are also the people with the most negotiating power. If you are offering people the old fast track or the slow track, that is no option for ambitious, success-minded people. They want to do the fast track their own way. And if you don't let them do it here, they will do it somewhere else."

One of the people in our meeting said, "The [heck] with them." He was genuinely insulted. Then they started talking among themselves, and one of them said: "This guy [meaning your author] has got a point. The best people do have a lot of negotiating power. We can afford a certain amount of attrition, but we need to slow it down. What we really need to focus on is keeping our very best people. But, you know what? We are not going to give in to the demands of the best people at the lowest end of the org chart. The most valuable people in this firm are the most experienced. We are the most valuable people in the firm. If we are going to create this kind of flexibility—work wherever, whenever, however you want—we should do that for the senior partners!"

This meeting was the genesis of a huge, meaningful initiative that marked a fundamental change that cascaded through many firms in the world of professional services. The typical retirement age for high-flying partners in big professional services firms is quite young, because the work is so grueling. Instead of having their most valuable people retire so young, the firm took the position of: "Restructure your job any way you want." Now, instead of losing many of their best, most seasoned partners, the firm would keep them available and on great terms indefinitely. They could be called upon when and where they are needed, and they will do the work at hand if they feel like it, negotiating appropriate fees for their services on an ongoing basis.

One time I was at Fort Leavenworth addressing a group of U.S. Army generals about best practices in retention of superstars. I told them how many business leaders are so concerned about turnover and so intent on not losing the training investment they make in their employees that they are going to great lengths to retain people in less-than-traditional ways.

I guess I wasn't thinking about my audience. Later, one of the generals said to me, "Son, when our employees go work for the competition, we shoot 'em."

But I learned something extremely valuable that day. The generals, I discovered, knew very well the value of the training investment they make in their soldiers, just as other employers do. The U.S. Army, however, has developed a very effective method of continuing to get a return on that investment long after soldiers finish their periods of service. The Army calls this method "the reserves." Why not borrow a staffing strategy for winning the talent wars from one of the greatest fighting forces in the history of the world? Build your own reserve army. You won't have the force of law to compel your former employees to return to service, but still, you can call upon your best former employees (those who have left on good terms, of course) when you need them. If they are available, they might return to help you, even it's for only one assignment. Or maybe they'll come back again.

If you stay in touch with your best former employees, they can sometimes turn out to be the backbone of a quick hiring strategy or a fluid staffing strategy. You've already trained them. They already know how to do business in your organization. They already know you and many of your colleagues, and probably plenty of your vendors and customers. Whose skill and performance abilities do you know better than those of the people who have already worked for you? When they come back, you'll probably have to fill them in on some new developments, but that's usually easily and quickly done.

Maybe, in the time they've been gone, they'll have discovered that the grass isn't that much greener on the other side. In some cases, before long, they'll be angling to get rehired again as full-timers. If you are smart, you'll let people flow back into your core group as easily as you let them flow out.

MANAGEMENT CHALLENGE #20:
WHEN YOU NEED TO MOVE A SUPERSTAR TO THE NEXT LEVEL TO DEVELOP AS A NEW LEADER

Managers ask me all the time about that superstar they are struggling to get to the "next level"—whatever that next level may be in this case.

On the one hand, this can be an internal struggle for the manager: if you succeed in getting that superstar to the next level, maybe you will lose her. Maybe the next level means not reporting to you anymore, either now or in the near future. Maybe it means the superstar will take on a new role, leaving a gap in her current role. You know the superstar is ready for the next level, but you may not be ready to give her up.

On the other hand, the struggle may be in convincing the superstar that the time is right for a new challenge. Maybe the superstar is comfortable thriving in his current role and the new role would be outside his comfort zone. Maybe the superstar is not eager to be put in charge of a group of his current peers. Maybe the superstar doesn't want to be exported to another group or location, even though it means a promotion and increased responsibilities. Maybe the superstar is not sure he's ready. Maybe he *is* not quite ready.

When this issue arises, managers often start asking about "transformational leadership." Is there such a thing? What is it?

Surely there are leaders—some great and some not—who contribute significantly to qualitative changes in the individuals and groups they lead. My view of transformational leadership is less romantic than most: I don't imagine the typical charismatic figure inspiring some deep, otherworldly commitment in employees. That happens but it is quite rare. In most real-world situations, transformational leadership is more accessible than the magical or profound version.

Real transformational leadership almost always occurs when a leader has taken the time to build a relationship of trust and confidence over a long period of time, through regular, high-quality communication. Not all long-standing one-on-one dialogues become transformational, of course. But I would argue that only the rarest of leadership relationships could possibly become truly transformational without first building on an extended period of regular, ongoing, high-quality communication. You have to take care of all the regular transactional aspects of the relationship first; remember, people are working first because they need to take care of themselves and their families. Second is the organization's mission and their ability to contribute to the mission. You have to take care of those two aspects—make sure the transactional relationship is running fair and square and smoothly—before you can hope to have a transformational effect on anyone.

When you have a superstar on your team, you need to move him out of his comfort zone and help him transform his role and take on the responsibilities of being a leader, build on that ongoing transactional relationship, and begin preparing him for the change. Move your relationship to the transformational level by focusing on preparing that superstar to grow.

Among the most challenging cases are when you have a technical superstar, someone who is really great at doing the nuts and bolts of the job, and you need that person to step up and become a manager. Sometimes it seems like it would require a transformation indeed to get your technical superstar to take on leadership responsibilities. How can you help that person step into that role successfully?

Here's what so often happens: the superstar who is best at her job (one of those with technical ability) is given more and more work. Over time, she needs people to help. As a result, she is given people to help and thus to supervise, often informally at first. Eventually she becomes a manager and may be taught how to complete the additional paperwork that comes with her new managerial responsibilities. But she is rarely taught *how* to be a manager. Instead, the superstar is forced to develop her own management style on an ad hoc basis, struggle, and finally conclude maybe she is not management material after all. Usually, though, she finds herself stuck in one situation after another, struggling with management responsibilities that nobody ever really taught her how to handle. So she goes through much of her career thinking, "I'm not a natural leader. I'm a . . ." (You fill in the blank: accountant, engineer, doctor, chef.)

The thing is, you want the superstar to be in charge of the team. She is best at the job, the one with the credibility and technical talent. Who is going to manage an accountant but an accountant? Who is going to manage a doctor but a doctor? Who is going to manage a chef but a chef?

When you are looking for new leaders, focus first and foremost on those with real technical talent, those superstars who are really good at their jobs and really into it. These are the individuals who have demonstrated their commitment to their work and careers. That commitment is the first essential piece when it comes to identifying new prospects for leadership roles.

What do new managers need most of all? They need support and guidance in learning and practicing the fundamentals of management. Make sure that the new manager is fully prepared to take on additional responsibilities and authority. Teach that new leader how to do the people work, and then support and guide her in this new role, in your regular one-on-ones, every step of the way:

- Remind the new leader regularly that this new role carries with it real authority, though of course it does not give her license to act like a jerk. It is a huge responsibility that should not be accepted lightly.

- Together, go over exactly what her new leadership responsibilities look like.

- Explain that management entails more than completing some extra paperwork. You have to explain the "people work" in detail.

- Create standard operating procedures for managing, and teach them to all new leaders. Focus on the fundamentals, like spelling out expectations for every employee who works for the manager, following up regularly, tracking performance closely in writing, and holding people accountable.

- When you formally deputize any new leader, no matter how small the project or how short the duration of the leadership role, announce the new leadership to the whole team, articulate the nature of this person's new authority, and explain the standard operating procedures for management that you have asked the new leader to follow.

- Check in daily (or every other day) with this new leader. Regularly walk through the standard operating procedures for managing people. Ask about the management challenges she is probably facing.

- Early on, you may want to sit in on the new leader's team meetings and one-on-ones with team members in order to build up her management skills and confidence. Do everything you can to reinforce her authority with the team and every individual on the team. But make sure to take every opportunity you can to help the new leader refine and improve her management techniques.

- Pay close attention every step of the way, and evaluate the new leader in her new role. Start focusing, in your regular one-on-one management meetings, on exactly how the new leader is doing the work of managing. Ask probing questions about each employee your manager is supposed to be managing: "When did you last meet with employee #1? What did you hope to accomplish? What did you talk about? What is #2 working on? What did #3 do last week? What guidance and direction did you give #4? What are #5's current goals and deadlines? What notes did you take down in your manager's notebook? May I take a look?"

- If you want your new manager to focus on something in particular with one or more of her employees, spell that out. If you want your manager to carry a specific message to their employees, hammer away at that message. Write it down. Put it on cards for your manager to hand out to employees. Talk it through. Role-play it.

- Of course, you'll also need to keep talking with your new leader about her nonmanagement responsibilities, but remember, every manager's first responsibility is managing. So that should be the number one priority in your managing of your managers.

With this kind of sustained, hands-on transactional leadership development effort and constant evaluation, you can actually have a transformational impact by developing this new leader.

I often joke with leaders and managers who are managing superstars: "Be nice to her. She might be your boss someday." Indeed, that happens more often than you might think. When you are managing superstars, remember, this is somebody you want to know forever. Be the kind of leader that superstar would never want to stop knowing.

CHAPTER SEVEN

The Challenges of Managing Despite Forces Outside Your Control

"How can I possibly meet the specifications and requirements when the specifications and requirements keep changing?"

"We don't have sufficient resources [tools, information, people, money, materials, space, time] to do the best possible job."

"I can't be expected to meet my deadline when I get another competing assignment from Ms. Otherboss or if I have to wait for Mr. Delay [in another team, department, or company for that matter] to give me the missing piece I need to proceed with my own part of the project."

These are just a few of the daily complaints managers hear from their direct reports. Of course, half the time, even as the manager, you have no more control over those things than your employees do. Not to mention the fact that you probably have to manage around a whole host of logistical hurdles depending upon how many people you manage, where and when they work, and how well you can understand each other. Managers often say,

"I can't control time and space! How can I maintain a high-structure, high-substance dialogue with sixteen [or sixty] direct reports? Or with employees in remote locations or different time zones, or working different schedules?"

"Some of my employees are from entirely different cultures or speak a different language from mine. How do I communicate clearly and appropriately with people whose language or culture I may not understand?"

If you are like most managers, you already spend time lobbying other managers at your level and above, including your boss or maybe even your boss's boss. You try to get final plans before your team digs in deep, try to hold off the change orders or at least keep them to a minimum. You constantly try to get your hands on more resources for your team. You regularly get on the phone to people in other departments and companies to cajole difficult counterparts when they are supposed to be cooperating with your employees. It feels very much like there is nothing you can do to obviate these forces outside your control:

- **Change** is a constant, and constant change is the new constant.
- **Competition for limited resources** is a constant, and perpetually constrained resources are the new constant.
- **Interdependency** is a constant—and increasingly unavoidable in today's complex world.
- **Technology** continues to expand the potential boundaries and parameters of management relationships, widening spans of control and making remote management increasingly common.
- **Globalization and diversity** is increasing the instances of working with people of different languages and cultures.

No matter what you do, you are not going to eliminate these external factors. You need to navigate through and around these factors and help your direct reports do so as well. Here's the problem: if you allow yourself to get caught in the wrestling match of trying to eliminate or obviate these unrelenting forces, you get distracted from the one thing you can control: your one-on-ones with your direct reports. Here's the irony: the more you try to eliminate or obviate the forces outside your control, the less time you have to spend with your direct reports. In this minefield of complexity, most employees need much more—not less—of your guidance, direction, support, and coaching. Yet the more complex the minefield, the more likely it is for the manager to be drawn away from his direct reports in order to negotiate with outside players on these external factors.

This is not quite as big a problem for a manager with one or two or three direct reports, especially if they are right there working alongside the manager much of the time. What if you have four or five or six, or sixteen, or sixty? You may well have direct reports who are working sometimes, or all of the time, in a different location from you or on a different schedule. You may have employees who don't speak the same language as you, or who are accustomed to a different culture. Yet you are no less likely to have to deal with the vagaries of constant change, constrained resources, and interdependency.

I hope, for your sake, that your situation is nowhere near as complex and difficult to control as that in the story I'm about to tell you.

A senior production manager (I'll call him "Skipper") ran a team of production engineers and technicians whose specialty was customizing highly sophisticated navigational systems for vehicles—mostly for military seacraft. They had a big order that required review by national security officials because it had military implications.

Skipper explains: "The approval process was on again, off again for two years, and it creates havoc for my team . . . Every time we get the green light, we ramp up and try to make progress. Then we get the word that the green light was really a yellow light. I'm trying to handle all this uncertainty and protect my team from it."

Meanwhile, I should add, Skipper's team of engineers and technicians was split physically between two production facilities. "Granted, they were only a few miles apart, but it just would have been so much easier for me if everybody was in one place."

Finally, the project received the necessary government approval to proceed, but the approval was contingent on replacing one of the components in the systems with an alternative component that was "less secret." This in turn caused their customer (the national government of a country in East Asia) to require that they obtain the alternative components from a designated supplier in this East Asian nation.

On top of all that, the language gap required the use of a translator. There were significant delays in getting the alternative components. When the shipment was finally delivered, the components were not right and had to be modified by technicians on Skipper's team.

Skipper says: "This production manager, through a translator, keeps telling me 'yes, yes, yes.' Then he comes right back and tells the guys on my team 'no, no, no.' So I'm back on the phone with him and he is saying 'yes, yes, yes.' Then he tells my guys 'no, no, no.'"

What was going on?

Skipper explains: "Finally one of my colleagues who had spent time in this country says to me, 'You are the boss. This is a very hierarchical, seniority-based society. The manager is trying to be polite and proper. It's not right in his culture for him to say "no" to you, because you are senior to him. So he calls your guys, who are on the same level as him, and says, "I told your boss 'yes' but really the answer is 'no.'"' When we finally got to communicate about the details, we were able to work it out."

This went on for several years. What did Skipper learn? He says:

I realized that I had spent a lot of time beating my head against the wall focusing on things that were totally out of my control. In the process, I was neglecting the area where I had the most control, which was keeping my team informed and involved. Most of the engineers and technicians insisted they were fine with all the change and all the hoops they had to jump through. They just hated feeling like they were in the dark a lot of the time. Instead of making them feel protected [and informed], I was unavailable, distracted, and they were left "in the dark." Once I got back in the swing of the regular one-on-ones, our internal communication improved dramatically. After that, they knew what I knew and that put them in a much better position to contribute to the planning and contingency planning. My mantra in those one-on-ones became, "Focus on what you can control."

We've seen a lot of evidence in our research to support Skipper's conclusion. When dealing with external factors outside your control:

1. *Focus on what you can control.* Instead of beating your head against the wall, figure out something you can actually do to make a difference, and then go do it.

2. As a leader, of course, you want to do everything you can do to protect and insulate your direct reports from the vagaries of uncertainty: change, resource constraints, interdependency, logistical challenges, differences in language or culture. But don't get so caught up in trying to protect and insulate your team that you end up unavailable and distracted, leaving them in the dark. *Stay vigilant with regular one-on-ones.* That is something you can control. And clear communication is even more critical than usual when you are in these situations.

Use your regular one-on-ones to keep your direct reports focused on what they can control, every step of the way.

MANAGEMENT CHALLENGE #21:
WHEN MANAGING IN AN ENVIRONMENT OF CONSTANT CHANGE AND UNCERTAINTY

"How can I possibly meet the specifications and requirements when they keep changing?" Some of your employees may come to you with this, and you may think they have a point. What do you do?

Change is nothing new. But there can be no doubt that the pace and scope of change is greater now than ever before. Just about everybody in today's workplace has his own stories of experiencing disruptive change and uncertainty, due to sources micro, macro, or both: climate change, natural disasters, globalization, technology, law, economics, culture, politics, trends, fads, weather patterns, moods, opinions, needs, desires.

People tell me every day about the pressure to adapt to changes at work: learning new skills, knowledge, wisdom; performing new tasks and responsibilities; fulfilling old tasks and responsibilities in new ways; working with new machines, new managers, new coworkers, new customers, new rules, new guidelines and parameters, new specifications and requirements. Usually the greatest difficulty for people is not coping with the changes, per se, but rather coping with the uncertainty. And being kept "in the dark" (like Skipper's crew).

It's up to you to keep your people out of the dark—to light the path forward, every step of the way, even if you have to do it just one or two steps at a time. The faster things change, the more you need to communicate. The more things are changing, the more often you need to communicate. In a constant-change situation, you need to be in constant communication—up, down, and sideways. You need to stay plugged in to your best sources of information through your own ongoing one-on-one dialogue with your boss, your direct reports, and key colleagues. Up, down, and sideways, you need to keep the lines of communication wide open in an environment of constant change.

How often do you need to meet with your people to keep them informed? As often as the pace of change requires. Every day? Twice a day? You need to reconnoiter—as a team, when it affects everyone, and in one-on-ones—and make it clear: "Here's what's changing. Here's what's staying the same. Here's what that means for you today. Here's what that might mean for you in the foreseeable future. Any questions?"

There is so much literature on "change leadership"—implementing lasting changes in systems, practices, and competencies—but not enough on leading people through incessant changes, large and small, that we couldn't stop if we tried. In the course of my work, I've come to know more than my share of what I call "change masters"—that is, leaders and managers with great track records of successfully leading direct reports through minefields of change (in some cases literal mine-fields). From these change masters I've learned what I call the three pillars of leading people through change:

1. Remind people constantly of whatever is constant. What is never going to change around here?
2. Engage in regular contingency planning with your people. What is likely to change? Exactly what will we do if that happens? Coach your people through practice runs of regularly recurring scenarios. What if "that" happens again? Exactly what will we do if "that" happens again?
3. When the unforeseen occurs, adapt and improvise. What else can you do?

What are your constants? What do you know for sure is not going to change any time soon? It's different in every organization and every team. Do you have rules, regulations, and procedures that can serve as rules of engagement for your direct reports? Standard operating procedures? In a high-change environment, one of the biggest favors you can do for your direct reports is to remind them regularly about all those things that are not going to change.

Once you know what is not going to change, then pretty much everything else is on the table. Of course, the toughest change to deal with is change that comes as if without warning. Unforeseen changes leave everybody scrambling to adapt and improvise. How many of these unforeseen changes should have been foreseeable? That's what contingency planning is for: trying to anticipate and prepare for changes in advance to deal with any number of scenarios that may or may not happen—that is, contingencies. If you are managing under conditions of great uncertainty or intense change, start building in regular contingency planning as part of your ongoing one-on-one dialogues. Talk about impending changes of which either of you are aware, for which you need to start preparing. Brainstorm risk factors for change. What are the forces likely to drive change that would directly affect you in the short term? Brainstorm foreseeable changes that could occur. What are the most likely contingencies? Start working together on step-by-step planning for the most likely contingencies:

- If A happens, you do 1, 2, 3, 4, 5.
- If C happens, you do 6, 7, 8, 9.
- If E happens, you do 11, 12, 13.

Focus in particular on regularly recurring scenarios. "That" happens a lot. When "that" happens again, exactly what should we do? Use what you know about regularly recurring scenarios to do practice runs through the scenario whenever possible. That's an especially good idea if you are managing a team whose members work together interdependently. Think of it as similar to practicing sports drills. Imagine you are a baseball team. Get together for infielding practice. Have your infielders practice turning double plays. If you have the opportunity, you should even run through entire "scrimmage" games.

One of my favorite change masters over the years was a longtime manager (I'll call him "Scrimmage") at a chain restaurant alongside a busy highway exit. Early in his tenure there, Scrimmage learned to "respect the arrival of a tour bus." Scrimmage told me: "One minute we are empty, the next minute we have eighty people who want to eat quickly." This is the equivalent of a battlefield situation in the restaurant industry. Scrimmage said, "It was a mess. We couldn't seat everybody. We couldn't get through half their orders. We had orders wrong. Food taking forever. And then they'd be gone. The drivers drove this route regularly, so they would not be inclined to come back, because they'd know we weren't really able to handle them.

"I had figured out, roughly, how much money we could make with a tour bus if we handled it well. I was determined and decided we were going to be great at that, at having eighty people just show up all at once. We came up with a playbook, basically. Then I would run my whole team through practice drills, like a scrimmage game." It worked.

His team got so good, the restaurant became known among quite a few tour bus drivers, who included it in their travel plans, in some cases even making a "reservation" of sorts, "usually between 3 and 4 P.M." His restaurant had the highest growth rate in the entire company that year, and their playbook became standard operating procedure for the entire chain when dealing with sudden bus group arrivals.

As a leader, you need to ask yourself: What kind of playbook do you have at your disposal to help your employees master things that are never going to change? The rules, regulations, and procedures? The best responses to regular recurring scenarios? Do they have a playbook? Do they get to practice together? Do they get to practice drills and scrimmages?

The best way for your employees to prepare to respond to the truly unforeseen is to learn and practice known best practices, step by step for as many of the contingencies as we possibly think up in advance. Over time, together, you and they will add more to that list. Employees who really get into contingency planning, playbooks, and scrimmaging will develop steadily growing repertoires of prepared responses. You are teaching them not just how to respond to changes, but also what it looks like and feels like to respond effectively to change.

Constant change is the new constant. It wasn't your idea. When circumstances change, requirements often change. That is just one more reason why you need to be highly engaged one person at a time, one day at a time, providing that guidance and direction every step of the way by asking:

- What's *never* changing around here? What are the constants?
- What *might* change sometime soon? What are all the ways we can prepare?
- What's changing *right now*?
- What's staying the same?
- What does that mean for you today, tomorrow, this week, next month?

MANAGEMENT CHALLENGE #22:
WHEN MANAGING UNDER RESOURCE CONSTRAINTS

"We don't have sufficient resources [tools, information, people, money, materials, space, time] to do the best possible job," say some of your direct reports, and you may think they have a point. What do you do?

Every assignment, task, or responsibility requires its own set of resources, and when resources are tight, competition for resources is fierce—both internally and externally. In today's workplace, you are being asked to do more and more with less and less: "We are raising the bar for your performance, but we are cutting your budget." The thing is, sometimes too lean is too lean. Without the necessary resources, your employees struggle to accomplish their jobs. Sometimes your employees don't have sufficient resources, and neither they nor you may even realize it until it's too late. There's no excuse for that.

Every time you assign a new project, task, or responsibility, you need to ask yourself: does this employee have the resources he needs to do the work assigned? Make resource planning a regular part of your regular one-on-one dialogue with every direct report.

Teach your direct reports to do a resource-needs inventory. Ask: "What are the primary resources you think you will need to accomplish the project or task in question?" This is a simple habit you can build into your ongoing management conversations. You need to talk through the resources your employee may want or need and which ones he will actually be able to obtain. He will need your guidance and direction. He might even need your direct help or intervention.

Based on our research, the following list covers just about any potential resource need one might need:

- Work space
- Supplies
- Materials
- Equipment
- Transportation

- Information
- Operation
- Maintenance
- People
- Talent
- Training
- Communication
- Cooperation

You can use this list as a tool to help you in your resource planning discussions. If the list doesn't work for you, then take a moment to think of the resources required for your direct reports to get their work done, then create your own list that you can use in your one-on-one management dialogue.

Whether you use the list here or one of your own creation, the one resource that you'll always need is time. To help your employees create their own comprehensive resource plans for every task, responsibility, or project assigned to them, you need to teach them to build in enough turnaround time for every resource acquisition. This means allowing enough time to prepare, receive, and process every resource request. Creating this timeline is critical, but most of the time, in order to create an accurate timeline for your resource planning, you'll need to teach your employees to do what I call "supply chain research."

Some resources are a whole lot easier to come by than others. Once you and your employee have determined what resources you will need, you need to figure out whether the resources are available, and if they are, from what source, at what cost, and with what process. If possible, have the employee do some research himself. Then talk through every aspect of the supply chain issues:

- What sources should he check to find out whether the resource is available?
- What process should he follow to get the resource?

- What turnaround time should he expect?
- What should he do in the event he runs into roadblocks?
- If there are resources that need to be purchased, this should be discussed in advance. If there is a budget and a purchase process, and your direct report needs to make purchases as part of his job, then you need to teach him how to work that process.

Teach your direct reports how to get resources in your organization. If there is a system internally, teach them how to work it. If there are key people they need to work with, make the introductions. The best thing you can do for your direct reports in a resource-constrained environment is to get them in the habit of making all their requests in the form of a simple proposal, which includes:

- What I propose
- The benefits: to whom, when, and by what measure
- The costs: to whom, when, and by what measure
- The schedule: Deadline and milestones along the way, plus how much of whose time and when that time would be required
- The plan: The steps along the way to each milestone, with key measures and time budgets

When managers teach their direct reports how to put their resource needs in the form of a simple proposal, employees tend to make many fewer requests and more reasonable requests in a much more thorough, persuasive, and professional manner. No matter how simple the process is, the very act of stopping to put their requests into a proposal format causes most employees to consider those requests more carefully. In the process, you are also teaching your direct reports to stop and think before they ask for anything.

If you succeed in teaching your direct reports to use proposals to get the resources they need, your team will be ahead of others when it comes to resources. When managers use this technique, their employees almost always get more resources for their own work or the work of their team; greater financial rewards for themselves or their subordinates; greater access to perks; credit for results achieved; new tasks, responsibilities, or projects; special assignments; training opportunities; and exposure to decision makers. One reason is that being forced to do a proposal leads employees to think through their needs more thoroughly, to allow more advance time, and to choose their battles more selectively. The second reason is that being forced to do a proposal leads employees to make their case much more persuasively.

What if you have direct reports who sometimes—or often—simply cannot get their hands on the resources they need to do their jobs optimally? Do you let them throw up their hands in frustration and declare, "There's nothing I can do!" If they don't have access to the resources they need to do the job, you need to teach them the art of the workaround, or a plan B.

Any successful person with significant work experience is quite familiar with the art of the workaround. In a pinch, without the necessary resources to do the job, your employees will be forced to come up with a workaround of one sort or another. Without your guidance and direction, the workaround might be tantamount to beating their heads against the wall trying to do something largely impossible, like digging a ditch with a salad fork. Or, without your supervision and support, they might go off wildly in another direction, causing unintended consequences. You don't want your direct reports winging it when they need to figure out a resource workaround. You want to help talk them through the process. Whenever possible, it makes sense to talk about potential workarounds well in advance, in the earliest stages of resource planning, and then continue the conversation every step of the way. As you help your direct reports anticipate necessary resources, discussing what sources to try and how they can go about getting the resources they need, you should also consider and talk through what to do if, despite best efforts, they are still not able to get the resources they need.

Talking Through the Four Steps of a Workaround

- *Step one.* Pursue an alternative source or supplier for your resource.

- *Step two.* Brainstorm possible substitutes for the resource you are having a hard time obtaining.

- *Step three.* Come up with an innovation—a method of completing the task that doesn't involve the resource (or even a reasonable substitute) you originally felt you needed. If you don't have the resources to do the job properly, you may have to devise a way to do the job differently. Maybe that different way of doing the job will be better.

- *Step four.* In the absence of a necessary resource, alternative source, substitute resource, or innovation, the only choice may be to employ much greater time and energy than originally intended. Don't underestimate the value of this, because so often it is the only workaround available. Try harder to get it done the hard way! If you can't find or fashion a vehicle, sometimes all you can do is run (or walk . . . or crawl). If you don't have rations, sometimes you just have to do the job hungry and thirsty.

Don't make the mistake of leaving your employees to their own devices to figure out how to get the resources they need to get their jobs done. It's critical that you engage your direct reports regularly to make sure they are planning for the resources they need and, especially, if they either cannot secure the resources they need on their own or must come up with a workaround or a plan B. You want to make sure to be part of that decision-making process every step of the way.

MANAGEMENT CHALLENGE #23:
WHEN MANAGING THROUGH INTERDEPENDENCY

"I can't be expected to meet my deadline when I get a competing assignment from Ms. Otherboss."

"I can't make my deadline because I have to wait for Mr. Delay [in another team, department, or company for that matter] to give me the missing piece I need to proceed with my own part of the project."

If you are like most managers, more and more of your work and probably that of your direct reports involves dealing with other people—internal and external. Most people must rely on the support and cooperation of many others in the course of doing their own work. In your regular one-on-ones, you need to coach your direct reports on how to navigate the complexities of interdependency. Interdependency is a two-part challenge:

1. *The "other boss"/"multiple bosses" problem*, when your direct reports answer to more than one boss and thus have to juggle competing assignments from other managers in addition to you.

2. *The "waiting for Mr. Delay" problem*, when your direct reports cannot complete their own assignments without the cooperation of individuals who are outside your immediate chain of command.

The "Other Boss"/"Multiple Bosses" Problem

It seems like everybody answers to so many people at work on a daily basis, sometimes it's hard for some of your direct reports to say exactly who is their actual boss. It's complicated for the employee and for you when you are managing an employee who answers to other bosses besides you. This direct report has more than one boss and/or dotted-line relationships on certain projects with other managers. When you give such an employee an assignment, it's not always clear how many other assignments that employee is juggling or whether an "urgent" assignment from another boss will interfere with completing an assignment on time for you. For his part, your direct report in this scenario is in a bit of a pickle. He needs to juggle the priorities of multiple competing bosses and either be worn to a frazzle or decide which one of you he is going to disappoint, if not both.

A senior partner in a large accounting firm (I'll call him "Mr. Tax") told me this story:

> We have constant competition among the partners and senior directors for the best associates. I could be working very well with an associate and then another partner would steal him

away. Then the associate is not delivering for me, because he is working for this other partner on something. So I'd talk to the associate and ask, "Did you tell [Mr. Otherboss] you were working on this project for me?" And he'd say, "Yes, I did, but I'm stuck in the middle." Here is this young associate trying to choose between the work I'm assigning and the work this other partner is assigning. How is the associate supposed to know how to set priorities in that case? Now I tell associates whenever I give them an assignment, "If another partner tries to give you an assignment, here's what I want you to do: tell him you are working on this for me with a tight deadline and that I told you [the associate] that you do not have the authority to put other assignments ahead of mine, so the other partner will have to call me to discuss the competing assignments." We [were putting] associates in that position all the time. It was not reasonable. It's up to me to provide that guidance about how to handle those conflicts.

You want to be the manager who provides guidance, direction, and support in helping your direct reports navigate their way through these complex authority relationships. Help your direct reports anticipate and plan for dealing with "other bosses" who might get in the way of your reporting relationship. In your regular one-on-ones, talk through the particular "other boss" scenarios that are getting in their way at any given point:

What if your own boss is one of those other bosses giving competing assignments to your direct reports?

Does your boss ever cut you out of the chain of command by going directly to your direct reports with assignments or instructions? Here's how to handle it:

1. Talk directly to your own boss about this. In your regular one-on-one with your boss, ask (in a pleasant, businesslike manner): "Did you mean to do that?" Then you have to ask (still in a pleasant, businesslike manner), "Are you now going to manage this employee on this assignment or instruction you've given, or do you want me to do

it? Do you want me to follow up with this employee? Would you like to make the assignment or instruction clear to me so that I can take it from here? Or are you going to take it from here? And are you taking over this employee altogether? Or do you want to share him with me?"

2. Teach your direct reports how to respond to your boss when he gives them assignments directly. Teach them to ask, "Do you want me to report to you on this assignment from now on or to my own manager? If I'm reporting to my own manager on this, maybe the three of us should discuss it together so we all have the same understanding of the assignment. If I'm reporting directly to you on this, maybe the three of us should discuss how it affects my other responsibilities."

3. Every step of the way, you (perhaps in dialogue with your boss), not your direct reports, should be deciding which of the competing assignments takes higher priority and make that 100 percent clear.

What if other "bosses"—dotted-line or internal customers or otherwise—are coming directly to your direct reports with competing assignments? Teach your direct reports to:

1. *Stop and check:* "Am I the right person for this assignment? Did you intend to choose me? After all, my primary assignments are X and my primary manager is Y."

2. *Determine the parameters of the assignment:* How long is this going to take? What are the requirements?

3. *Figure out whether this assignment will get in the way of their primary assignments.* But don't make excuses. Simply explain the conflict and ask when they need to get back to the other manager.

What if other bosses hold your direct reports to higher or lower standards than you or impose conflicting rules?

1. Always make sure your direct reports are 100 percent clear about the standards you expect from them when they are reporting

to you. The more "other bosses" your direct reports have, the more opportunities there are for conflict and confusion. So it becomes important to remind those direct reports regularly of your standards and rules. Let them know, "Whenever you are working on an assignment for me, we follow these standards and these rules. On this assignment, here are the standards. Here are the rules. Are we clear?" Whenever possible, provide a set of standard operating procedures, step-by-step instructions, or a checklist.

2. Remind your direct reports that when they are working for other managers, they need to get 100 percent clear on the standards that the other manager expects when they are reporting to her. Tell your direct reports, "When you are working for me, please do it my way. When you are working for that other manager, do it her way." Unless, of course, another manager is asking your direct reports to do something that is outright wrong or bad. Teach them in such a case to come to you immediately for your help.

I knew a longtime media executive who had this approach to competing with other bosses for his direct reports' time and effort: "If an employee reports to me and another honcho too, you can be sure, I am definitely the executive that employee does not want to disappoint. I make sure of that!" Why don't they ever want to disappoint him? He followed these simple, clear rules of engagement:

- Be the manager who is always going to follow up and insist on accountability.

- Be the manager who sets up employees for success and tracks their performance and follows through with credit and rewards accordingly when they deliver.

- Be the manager who pays close attention to what other projects your employee is juggling for other managers. Ask lots of questions about her other tasks and deadlines. Talk about how your assignment might interfere with her other work. Ask how her other work might interfere with the work you are assigning. Decide together whether she will be able to meet your requirements. Make a plan for how she will respond if any other responsibility interferes with meeting your deadline or meeting your requirements.

• Be the manager who holds everybody to a high standard, regardless of what other managers require. Remind your employees regularly and enthusiastically that you are different.

"Waiting for Mr. Delay"

It can be very frustrating when you are managing an employee whose work requires that he wait for another individual to finish some piece of the puzzle before he can complete his tasks. Your employee could, would, should be done. But he is waiting for Mr. Delay to deliver his piece of the puzzle.

Of course, so often the resource your direct report needs is just a piece of information, a number, ten words, a document, or an approval. What your direct report really needs in each of these cases is the regular (or occasional), informal (or formal) cooperation and assistance of another person, internal or external, who is probably outside your direct chain of command.

You need to provide guidance and direction to help your direct report learn to get what he needs from these key counterparts—how to identify the right people in the right places and develop strong, mutually supportive working relationships with them.

In your one-on-one management dialogue, talk through with every direct report and anticipate together what cooperation and assistance he might need from other colleagues—internal and external—to get their projects, tasks, and responsibilities done. Talk through the following questions:

• Exactly who should they ask for, what, when, and how?
• What is the precise nature of the working relationship with each person on whom they may need to rely?

- What level of cooperation and assistance is appropriate and reasonable to request?
- In each case, is there more than one person to whom your direct report could turn for cooperation and assistance? What should he do if he is having trouble getting cooperation and assistance from one person or another?

Over time, by talking through these issues on a regular basis in your one-on-ones, you can teach your direct reports to develop "go-to people" in all the key areas where they have recurring interdependency needs. Go-to people are the people you know you can go to when you need something. They are people you can rely on. They are responsive and effective. They get things done. What is the secret to developing good working relationships with go-to people? One of the greatest networkers I've ever known, a titan of executive search, taught me years ago: "If you want to be able to go to go-to people, then you have to become a go-to person yourself. Go-to people need go-to people too. It's reciprocal, 'mutual go-to-ism.'"

Teach your direct reports to become go-to people so that they can develop reciprocal go-to relationships with other go-to people. How should your direct reports go about this? Teach them to bend over backward to do things for other people, to be reliable, responsive, and effective. Teach them to get things done. Deliver on commitments. And teach them to conduct themselves always in a professional manner with a great attitude. They will develop reputations.

Meanwhile, how can your employees do business with Mr. Delay (decidedly not a go-to person) more effectively? Teach your direct reports:

- In the absence of direct authority, your only option is to use influence. Conduct yourself always in a businesslike, professional manner. Be the person Mr. Delay does not want to disappoint. Influence through persuasion. Use good reasons to convince Mr. Delay to deliver: "This is why you should do this for me. This is why it's a good thing for you, your team, and your company. This is why you should put my request first. This is why nothing else should get in the way."

- Influence through facilitation: do everything possible to help support and assist Mr. Delay's fulfillment of his part. What are all the things you can do to make it easier for Mr. Delay to deliver?

- Make specific commitments. Clear timelines for deliverables with reminders along the way are more likely to be fulfilled.

There are two instances when a manager should intervene to help a direct report get Mr. Delay's cooperation. One is if the direct report is getting zero response despite following the best practices just detailed. The second is if Mr. Delay is such a VIP that the direct report really should not risk pushing too hard.

If you've been teaching your direct reports these best practices for managing interdependency, keep discussing them in your one-on-ones. Consider how well your employee is learning to handle the people she depends on to accomplish her tasks. Meanwhile, what are your direct reports supposed to do while they are waiting for Mr. Delay? Teach them to:

- Focus on the tasks they can accomplish on their own, without Mr. Delay or anyone else. Together, talk through all the steps they can and should take, leading up to the point where they have to rely on someone else. When they have done so, evaluate how well they accomplished those tasks.

- Make a plan to reduce downtime, maintain productivity, and continue moving the project along. Together, talk through exactly what you expect them to do during that waiting period.

You simply cannot hold an employee accountable for the action or inaction of another person outside your chain of command. Don't let your employees be held up by Mr. Delay. Help them learn to handle these difficult situations and keep the work moving forward by staying focused on concrete actions that are within the employees' control.

MANAGEMENT CHALLENGE #24:
WHEN MANAGING AROUND LOGISTICAL HURDLES

Recall the common manager dilemmas voiced earlier in the chapter:

> "I can't control time and space! How can I maintain a high-structure, high-substance dialogue with sixteen [or sixty] direct reports? Or with employees in remote locations or different time zones, or working different schedules?"

If you are going to conduct a regular, ongoing one-on-one dialogue with every single direct report, there are some basic logistical details to consider. You need to figure out exactly who you will be meeting with, where, when, for how long, and how often.

Even in the easiest of circumstances, maintaining an ongoing dialogue with every person requires organization, planning, and rigorous and disciplined follow-through. And how many people are working under the easiest of circumstances? More likely, you are managing around one or more logistical hurdles. Maybe you have too many people to manage, or you are trying to manage people in remote locations or who work a different schedule than yours.

Whenever a manager tells me, "I have too many people to manage," my first reaction is this reality check: Do you really have thirteen or thirty people who directly report to you? Or do you have a chain of command; that is, employees who are actually managers, supervisors, or team leaders who are supposed to be managing some of the other employees in your group?

If you have a chain of command, you must use it effectively. Make a habit of talking to these supervisors or team leaders every day and focus intensely on helping them play the role you need them to play. Teach them how to manage on an ongoing basis, and manage how they manage every step of the way. Just as you are working hard to be a strong manager, they need to do the same.

If you don't have a chain of command, maybe you should establish one. There is no magic number for how many direct reports a manager can handle. But surely there is a limit. If you have thirty people, you simply cannot afford to be the only leader on the team. Cultivate and develop high performers who are in your inner circle, who share your priorities and help you keep the team focused on the work at hand. Developing new leaders, even informally, will help you extend your reach; you can use them as temporary project managers and deputize them when you are not available. But don't give anyone management responsibilities of any kind—formal or informal—unless you are prepared to focus on that leader intensely and personally manage that leader's management practices very closely.

No matter how many people you are responsible for managing, you will have to make choices every day about how you are going to use your dedicated management time. Concentrate on four or five people every day. Some employees will need more time than others. But don't just talk to the winners and the losers. Talk to everybody in between. Maybe take one employee from the high end, one from the low end, and a third from the middle—each day. That's fifteen a week. Thirty every two weeks.

What about managing employees who are working on a different schedule from you? Or maybe your employees are working on the other side of the planet in an entirely different time zone. Even if they are just across town, they may be working on a different schedule. What do you do?

These scenarios present the same logistical issues as those working in remote locations. In all of these cases, you need to establish with that employee (I'll call him "Remote") a protocol for maintaining well-functioning ongoing one-on-one dialogue:

• Keep each other informed about when you'll both be at a central location, such as the organization's headquarters, so you can schedule in-person one-on-one time.

- Schedule occasional in-person meetings when it is convenient for you to visit Remote or when it is convenient for Remote to visit you in your location.

- If you have even simple video phone capability, consider meeting sometimes via video phone.

- In the absence of in-person meetings and two-way web cams, you have to make certain to make good use of regular telephone and electronic communication. Too often managers of Remotes slip into management by interruption and "call me when you need me." As a result, their communication becomes increasingly disorganized, incomplete, and random. Until, of course, something goes wrong, and then they find themselves managing by "firefighting."

- Schedule regular one-on-one telephone calls with Remote, and never miss the calls.

- Prepare in advance of your one-on-ones and ask Remote to prepare too. It is often a good idea to ask Remote to prepare a written recap of highlights and key issues since your last one-on-one call, as well as open questions to discuss during the one-on-one. Also, Remote should send for your review, in advance, any work in progress that is going to be discussed.

- Immediately following each call, ask Remote to send you an email recapping what you both agreed on in your conversation—the actions Remote is expected to take, the steps Remote will follow, and the timeline, as well as the date and time of your next scheduled phone call—and ask Remote to prepare in advance and send any documents for review prior to the next meeting.

Sometimes when I teach these best practices in my seminars, someone will raise a hand and say, "My employees work across the hall from me, but a lot of our relationship is conducted by telephone and email nonetheless." Indeed. Our research shows that conducting face-to-face conversations—whenever possible—is much better than conducting your management conversations solely by telephone and electronic communication. However, electronic communication has a built-in advantage: when you and your direct reports are communicating electronically, you are creating a paper (or electronic) trail. Save those emails and you'll have record of your ongoing dialogue with this direct report. If the emails are organized and thorough, Remote might be able to even print them out and use them as checklists, or use them as the basis for crafting work plans, schedules, to-do lists, and other tools to help guide him in his work. For your part, *you* can use that paper trail as part of your ongoing tracking and documentation of this employee's performance.

MANAGEMENT CHALLENGE #25:
WHEN MANAGING ACROSS DIFFERENCES IN LANGUAGE AND CULTURE

Here's another common manager dilemma from the chapter opening:

> "Some of my employees are from entirely different cultures or speak a different language from mine. How do I communicate clearly and appropriately with people whose language or culture I may not understand?"

In an increasingly global and culturally diverse workforce, it is more and more common for managers to find themselves engaging in dialogues with employees who are accustomed to different cultural norms, not to mention people who do not even speak the same language as the manager. It's hard enough when you don't speak the same *cultural* language as your employees, when you must accommodate different assumptions, points of reference, and communication practices. But how can you maintain a regular ongoing dialogue with an employee when you literally don't speak the same language?

In many organizations—such as global businesses, the military, intelligence organizations, foreign service, or global aid circles—crossing culture and language barriers is just part of the job. If you go to work for the Peace Corps or the CIA, they are going to give you a crash course in the language and culture of wherever it is they are going to send you, before they send you. While you are there, they will provide translators and guides whenever possible as well as translation aids. And in your own organization, that's pretty much all you can do, too:

- Take a crash course in a nation's language and culture.
- Use a translator or guide whenever you can.
- Use translation tools.

These are the simple best practices used by people in organizations with all the resources in the world. I've also seen them used by managers with very few resources in industries such as health care, agriculture, landscaping, restaurants, and construction.

A highway construction manager (I'll call him "Highway") used these practices with his road crew chiefs and team leaders when managing employees who were not English language speakers. Highway said: "You need to have someone on the crew who speaks both languages. You need a translator." Second, do the crash course. "Lots of the guys on the crew speak Spanish. Over the years, some of the team leaders have learned a little bit of Spanish, enough to get by, and we encourage these guys to start learning some English too." Even if you don't learn each other's language, *you* can maybe start to build up some shared vocabulary, maybe a combination of both languages, that you can use to communicate about the work at least. "It's got to be enough to communicate what needs to be done." The real innovation in their approach was creating checklists in two (and sometimes three) languages. That way, the crew chiefs, team leaders, and employees could use the checklists as translation tools. "They could actually point to items on the checklist, and then they would all understand." That also helped everyone learn a lot of key terms in one another's language and also made sure that all of their conversations revolved around those checklists, which is a pretty nice bonus.

It may be pretty obvious that you cannot manage an employee if you and that employee cannot understand each other at all due to a language barrier. Cultural barriers can be just as great, although sometimes they are much less obvious. Managers tell me all the time, "At long last, I came to realize I had been misreading this employee" or "This employee had been misreading me." When a large, well-resourced employer sends you overseas to another part of the world, they are probably going to spend some time making sure you are prepared. On the other hand, when you have one or more employees from different cultural backgrounds, there is probably no formal support or training for that. You are expected to just decode those differences on your own. How do you go about that?

One place to start is by learning from the best practices of the large and well resourced. One globetrotting IT executive (I'll call him "Global") who has worked in senior roles in numerous top tier multinational organizations shared this with me: "Thirty years ago, when I did my first posting abroad, they gave us an intensive orientation program. It was six weeks. A real deep dive into the people, the place, the culture. We spent a lot of time on customs and communication. We also had locals who were available to answer questions and act as guides the whole time we were there." How did it work? Global says, "It gave us a huge advantage over other people in the expatriate business community. You could just tell that very few people had that level of preparation that we had received or had that degree of local support that we had. It was obvious they were at a big disadvantage, not just socially but in terms of their effectiveness. Based on that first posting abroad, I've always made sure that I and every one of my team get the cultural education and support necessary to succeed."

What if you don't have access to a well-resourced orientation program? Then you have to construct a deep-dive learning experience for yourself. Get books. Watch movies and documentaries. Talk to people. Do whatever you can to prepare.

Now Global is based back in North America but is managing a globally dispersed team, with truly globally diverse personnel. Global has been using his experience and wisdom to help guide the team in understanding and appreciating each other's differences. "When you are working closely with someone day after day who has very different cultural assumptions, there is a lot of room for misunderstanding. It is worth knowing where that person is coming from so you can avoid unnecessary misunderstandings. Just as if we were all going to go work in India, the fact that 60 percent of our employees are in India or from India means obviously we all need to do a deep dive on India. Just as they need to do a deep dive on North America."

You can use this deep-dive approach to bridge any sort of cultural diversity gap on your team. Global told me this great story: "I now have two teams that are almost entirely made up of early twenty-somethings. As far as I'm concerned, they are not just from another culture, it's like they are from another planet." This is a matter of generational diversity. Global continues: "So now I'm doing a deep dive on this generation. I've been reading books and doing research. I've been talking to some of my team about it as well. I told a couple of them they are to be my mentors on this deep dive. They are going to be my cultural guides to this new generation."

What if you don't have a critical mass of people from one "foreign" culture (or generation)? What if it's just one person? Do you need to be a bit of an anthropologist even if you have only one foreigner on your team?

I'll answer that with another question: Exactly which one of your employees are you thinking is *not* at least just a little bit different? Every single one of your direct reports is different from the rest in ways that are more and less obvious. All of your employees come to work with different levels of ability and skill: different backgrounds, personalities, styles, ways of communicating, work habits, and motivations.

Treat every single person as if he is from a different culture. Do a deep dive on everybody. If you don't already know what makes one of your employees a little bit different, maybe it's time to figure that out. Every step of the way, you are looking for the right words, tone, gestures, style, and customs to connect and communicate about the work. And that's the really good news: no matter how much difference there may be between and among your direct reports, there is one thing they always have in common. That is the work. The work is what's bringing all these very different people together. Every step of the way, keep everybody focused on the common ground:

- Who is going to do what, where, when, and how?
- Here are the broad performance standards.
- Here are the expectations.
- Here's a checklist for every expectation.

Then monitor, measure, and document performance every step of the way. Follow up. All differences can ultimately be resolved based on a simple formula: which option will result in getting more work done, better and faster?

CHAPTER EIGHT

The Challenges of Management Renewal

What if you are not the new leader on the scene in any way whatsoever, but you wish you could start some or all of your management relationships anew?

So often managers tell me, "I can see now that I should be a strong, highly engaged manager, but I've been in this role managing many of the same people for years on end." These managers often ask: "How can I possibly just change my management style one day?"

Often these are long-standing workplace relationships. So the employees in question are accustomed to the way they've always interacted with this manager. If you make a big change, they are going to feel it. They might even challenge you on the legitimacy of your change effort or doubt the likelihood of your success.

That's why I always tell managers not to rush into a big change in your management relationships. Keep in mind that becoming a strong manager is not about putting your foot down, but rather much more like taking a walk every day. You need to be in this for the long haul if it's going to work. So stop and think. Make sure you are ready psychologically. Make sure you are ready tactically. Make sure you have made all the preparations necessary.

It takes guts to make a big change; that's true whether you are considering a wholesale renewal of your management style or just a renewal of one or more specific management relationships.

Start strong. The new beginning is your best opportunity to reestablish the ground rules for your working relationship. This is your chance to create a new clarity and alignment:

- This is our mission.
- This is our work in relation to the mission.
- This is how we operate from now on.
- These are our standards. This is how I'm going to operate from now on.
- This is what I'm going to do to help you from now on.
- This is what I have to offer you in return.

First and foremost, that means dedicating the time for high-structure, high-substance team meetings and regular, ongoing one-on-one dialogues starting on day one of your renewal. Take heart. Remember, this is good news. Remember the "Good news!" management speech from Chapter Two? Think about it: you are about to let your people know that you are making a new commitment to practicing the fundamentals of management. How can anyone on your team truly object when you say: "I'm going to be stronger and more highly engaged from now on"? Craft your own message with the key elements of the "Good news!" message:

- I am going to try to live up to the huge responsibility of leadership.
- I'm going to spell out expectations for you and help you plan your work.
- I'm going to track performance.
- I'm going to help you learn, get tools and resources, solve problems, and earn more.

Perhaps the toughest part of renewal is sticking with it. Like any change in habits, it's not easy to stay on the wagon. For a leader with long-standing relationships, it could be very tempting to fall off the wagon and go back to your old management habits. So you have to be diligent and vigilant for weeks or months or sometime longer before the changes really become the new normal.

Every step of the way, keep asking yourself:

- Who needs to be managed more closely?
- Who needs more responsibility and autonomy?
- Who needs help navigating the complex, ever-changing workplace?
- Who needs help with the fundamentals of self-management?
- Who needs performance coaching to speed up or slow down?
- Who has a great attitude, and who needs an attitude adjustment?
- Who is likely to improve? Who is not?
- Who should be developed? Who should be fired?
- Who are the best people? Who are the real performance problems?
- Who requires special accommodations and rewards? Who deserves them?

Yes, consistency is critical. But even more important is knowing what to do when you fall off of the strong-leadership wagon for a while. Don't beat yourself up if you miss a day or a week or a month or years. Just stop and think. Prepare yourself. And then get right back to being strong and highly engaged. One person at a time. One day at a time.

MANAGEMENT CHALLENGE #26:
WHEN YOU NEED TO RENEW YOUR MANAGEMENT RELATIONSHIP WITH A DISENGAGED EMPLOYEE

"I've got this one employee who is just not 'into it.' Everybody else is on board, but somewhere along the way, I lost him, and I've had a very hard time getting him back on board."

I hear about this one disengaged employee (I'll call him "Eeyore") from managers of every sort. My first response is always the same: "How often are you having one-on-ones with Eeyore?" More than half the time, the manager's answer is something like: "I have one-on-ones with everybody regularly, except for Eeyore." Well, no wonder Eeyore is disengaged!

The manager usually explains: "The one-on-ones with Eeyore were like pulling teeth. He would miss them or come unprepared or be unresponsive. The one-on-ones seemed to make him even less engaged, not more. Over time, I have to admit, I've let the one-on-ones with Eeyore slip. We don't have them very often anymore."

The problem here is not that the employee is disengaged. The problem is that the manager has disengaged from the employee. Of course, that is until a problem comes up that can no longer be ignored. And by that time, the conversations are not likely to go well, especially with Eeyore, especially if the manager has not been engaging in regular one-on-one conversations about Eeyore's work. Yet no matter how painful those regular one-on-ones might be with the disengaged employee, they are a whole lot less painful than the inevitable confrontation that is likely to ensue when the inevitable problems do occur.

The regular one-on-one is the only medicine in this case. But sometimes you have to be prepared to give it in doses over a long period of time. The medicine takes longer with some than with others. Almost always, eventually, even some of the most stubborn will respond, once they realize the one-on-ones are going to keep happening, like the sun coming up every morning. Perhaps the very most stubborn employees will decide they want no part of the regular one-on-ones, but at least they will realize that the only way to escape the one-on-ones is to escape from you altogether. So be it.

Be honest with yourself. Have you let yourself and Eeyore off the hook here and, in the process, convinced yourself it is all Eeyore's fault? If the answer is yes, just go back to having the one-on-ones. Do not stage an intervention. Do not make proclamations like, "Eeyore, I'm putting my foot down! We are going to have these conversations come heck or high water!" Eeyore may well feel attacked or confronted. He may feel you are blaming him for the inconsistency of the one-on-ones to this point. This may come as a shock, seemingly without warning, especially when the failure to do the one-on-ones has been going on for a while and it is really a conspiracy in which you are both complicit. Eeyore is thinking, "I thought we had an understanding. I don't really do the one-on-one thing." Meanwhile, Eeyore is likely to feel demoralized. There are bad feelings. After all that, the one-on-ones will be more difficult than ever.

If you find yourself in this situation, don't blame the employee! Instead, take full responsibility. You are the manager. It is your job to make sure those one-on-ones are happening regularly and consistently every step of the way, no matter how unpleasant it may be. If you haven't been doing the one-on-ones with Eeyore, just start doing them again.

I remember very well a situation like this, involving the manager of a shipping supply warehouse (I'll call her "Ms. Shipp") with two longtime employees who were resistant to Ms. Shipp's efforts to manage them. Ms. Shipp had long been making the classic mistake with Eeyore and Grumpy. Ms. Shipp said: "Trying to have regular one-on-ones with them was more trouble than it was worth. With Eeyore and Grumpy, the one-on-ones were always in fits and starts. They never really became routine with either one of them. They would just sort of go away, and we would talk only as needed."

Was that a problem? "For one thing, other employees wondered why Eeyore and Grumpy didn't have regular one-on-ones with me, especially since they were not exactly the best employees. Also, since I was less involved in their work, I had a lot more unwelcome surprises in those areas.

"The longer I accepted the situation, the less I felt justified in making big changes in how I was managing the two of them. But I finally got fed up with the situation and decided I had to start holding *myself* to a higher standard as a manager. I had to start managing these two like I was managing everybody else!"

Did Shipp stage an intervention, or blame the employees? She says, "I told them, 'It's not you, it's me. Shame on me for not being a better manager for you. Shame on me for not insisting that we have regular one-on-ones just like I do with everyone else. I will not make that mistake again. I promise to do better. Let's schedule our next one-on-one, and I promise we will have them from now on like clockwork.'"

Were they surprised? Yes. Did they believe Shipp would stick with the plan this time? Maybe not right away.

In becoming a strong, highly engaged leader, you too may have weak moments, weak days, weeks, even months. As hard as you try, you will sometimes drop the ball with one or two of your employees, sometimes more. Your employees will notice. Then it may be really hard to start managing again after being disengaged for some period of time. After all, you are human. Just try to bounce back sooner rather than later. One mistake managers make is they feel so guilty and sheepish after going through a rough patch that they remain disengaged much longer than they should. If you've been disengaged, have fallen out of your hands-on routine, or are off schedule, the only thing to do is to get back on schedule and into your routine as fast as possible. Acknowledge your failure in your discussions with your employees. Promise to do better.

Looking back, Ms. Shipp realized: "As soon as we were back in those regular management conversations, I began to have that dedicated time to require them to engage. As soon as it became clear that the one-on-ones were not going away this time, the two of them became a study in contrasts." Eeyore gradually got used to the one-on-ones and began to cooperate more and more. "It was like an upward spiral." On the other hand, Grumpy dug in his heels and simply refused to participate. He would sit through the one-on-ones with his arms crossed. It wasn't too long—a couple of months—before Grumpy decided to take another job working for a different manager in a different operation in the warehouse. Was that good for the company? No. Was that good for Ms. Shipp? She says, "Yes, it was a decent outcome for me. At least I didn't have to deal with him anymore. And with

Eeyore on board and really contributing more than ever, I didn't even fill Grumpy's position, and we never missed a beat."

Without the regular one-on-ones, you have no venue in which to require engagement. The one-on-ones are your regular, recurring opportunity to relentlessly provide the employee with the regular evaluation and feedback about the work—good, bad, or neutral—and to require him to report verbally and in writing on exactly how his performance is lining up with expectations. Exactly what did he do? What is he doing? What is he planning to do next? When an employee resists that process, you need to stick to it. When you slip, you need to get back to it. In those one-on-ones, you require engagement: If an employee refuses to report to you appropriately in these one-on-ones, then he is failing at his job, plain and simple. If he does report to you appropriately in these one-on-ones, then he is engaging as much as you can require. Take that for what it's worth and try to use those one-on-ones to build on that engagement, one day at a time, until it becomes an upward spiral.

Exactly how did Ms. Shipp build that upward spiral with Eeyore? She says, "I wanted him to have a feeling of success right away so that he would feel better about the job, about me, about our working relationship. In every one-on-one, I set up small wins that were easy for him to get. They were right there within his reach, just in doing his regular job, but I laid out one very small 'extra' for him in every one-on-one. Each time I made sure it was an extra that was easy for him to reach. That way, he was banking one small win after another. In every one-on-one I got to thank him and congratulate him on his success and then set up another very easy challenge." Was it just an illusion of success Ms. Shipp was creating? "I just basically gave him one extra thing to do twice a week. After a couple of months, that really added up. It made everybody's work easier, including his own." She explained, "That's why I say it was an upward spiral. Each little success created more success."

What if you have a disengaged employee who neither takes to the upward spiral nor does you the favor of self-destructing like Grumpy? What if your employee's disengagement resists the medicine of aggressive and persistent one-on-ones? This may be the sort of problem I deal with in Chapter Five on attitudes (one of the classic "bad" attitudes, a conflict on the team, or a personal problem at home). Or it could be the sort of problem I deal with in Chapter Three on self-management (for example, the employee may need work on interpersonal communication skills). I'm not talking about those issues here. Here, I'm talking about the sort of issue Ms. Shipp had in the very stubborn employee, Grumpy, who simply refuses to engage.

What do you do if Grumpy doesn't solve your problem for you by deciding to leave on his own? You need a plan for using your regular one-on-ones to give this employee one last chance to succeed.

1. *Review your notes from previous one-on-one meetings.* Make sure you have all the pertinent details: dates and times that Grumpy has failed to take specific actions to meet the expectations you've been setting every step of the way.

2. *Consider your role in Grumpy's performance problem.* Are you confident you've done a thoughtful and thorough job of trying to help this person improve? Did you spell out expectations clearly every step of the way? Did you monitor and measure fairly and accurately every step of the way? Have you given this person every opportunity to improve? Have you documented all of this clearly every step of the way? Before you proceed, consult an ally (or make a brand-new one) in HR. Make sure you are following proper procedures before you have this performance intervention.

3. *Prepare thoroughly.* Create a script so you stay on track during the conversation. Anticipate any excuses the employee typically offers you for failing to improve performance. During the conversation, make sure you:

- Clarify that you are meeting to discuss a problem.
- Confront the employee in direct terms, letting her know that her failure to improve her performance is unacceptable.
- Present the facts as you've documented them; be as specific as you can be.

- Share a list of nonnegotiable action items that the person must complete within a specific time frame.
- Establish that failing to resolve the performance problem, whatever that might be, will result in negative consequences for the employee.

4. *Follow through.* If an employee fails to improve his performance, despite your regular coaching and putting him on warning, at some point you simply have to start imposing real negative consequences. Beyond that, the only place to go is letting the employee know that his job is on the line. Whether and when to fire an employee is always a tough decision. If you've monitored, measured, and documented his performance every step of the way, you will be in a much better position to make the right decision. Firing people is often not easy in an organization. You usually have to jump through hoops first. Your organization has a process for firing an employee. Learn the rules. Follow the rules. Work the rules. And ask for help from your boss, other managers, HR, and your company's legal department.

MANAGEMENT CHALLENGE #27:
WHEN YOU NEED TO RENEW YOUR OWN COMMITMENT TO BEING A STRONG, HIGHLY ENGAGED MANAGER

Managers tell me all the time: "I've been managing the same people for some time now. I realize now that I've been too hands-off. Is it even possible to change my whole management style after all this time? How can I get my employees to take me seriously? How can I avoid them thinking I've bought into some gimmicky 'flavor of the month'?"

Let your employees think whatever they want in the beginning. You can live with anybody's doubt but your own. Step one in convincing your employees will be your own belief in the change and your determination to stick with it. Over time, the doubts will recede and the doubters will come along or else move along. That's why you cannot afford to make a halfhearted effort at change. You are better off making no change at all than a halfhearted effort. But it takes more than a full heart to succeed.

I've seen many full-hearted efforts fail due to a lack of preparation. A well-meaning manager who decides to become a better manager can painfully underestimate the challenge of making a big change in management style, especially after a long period of weak management. Often the manager in question has read a book or been to a seminar. I often receive emails from managers: "I'm ready! I'm eager! I'm going to become a strong, highly engaged manager!" My first response is always: "Wait! Step back! If you are really sure you want to do this, don't take it lightly. This is going to be a big change. Take some time to prepare." More often than not, the response is something like: "You don't understand. I've already started!!" Typically, the manager says, "If all that's missing is the fundamentals, I might as well just jump in and start." (Ah, yes—and yet, isn't mastering the fundamentals in any field a lifelong enterprise for even the greatest practitioners?)

One such manager I remember well—a senior manager in an environmental consulting firm (I'll call her "Ms. Green")—told me, "I'm going to start meeting with my employees one-on-one starting tomorrow! I've scheduled thirty-minute one-on-ones with all of them, and I've got my manager's notebook all set so I can take notes during all the one-on-ones. I'll let you know how it goes." Of course, Ms. Green did not realize that her employees were taken by surprise. Some were in a minor panic. What on earth did she want to talk to all of them about, one-on-one, the next day? Were people going to be fired? Was she leaving? What was happening?

The morning came, the one-on-ones ensued, nobody was fired, and there was no earth-shattering announcement. Ms. Green's direct reports realized that she was just trying a new approach to managing. By the end of the day, everybody was murmuring: "She read that book. This is just the flavor of the month. Sit tight. It will go away soon. She won't stick with it." When Ms. Green shared this with me, I sent a note back to her: "Will you or won't you? That's entirely up to you."

Ms. Green was inspired and committed, but she had launched her change effort without sufficient preparation. She had underestimated the impact of the change on herself, her role, her experience at work, and her relationships with her direct reports, with her own boss, and even with some of her colleagues. She had also failed to fully appreciate just how much her employees really needed her, once she started actually talking regularly with them, one-on-one, for a few weeks. She told me, "I am stunned at just how often I am able to see a problem and help one of my employees avoid it. How often I can see a better way to do something—sometimes it's something they've been doing wrong for years."

She was incredibly busy to begin with, and she quickly began to realize that managing more closely is time-consuming, especially at first. Some employees were pushing back and complaining that Ms. Green was "all of a sudden micromanaging"; some thought she was "picking on them and favoring others." There was a lot of tension in the air. Then Ms. Green started getting a little heat from her own boss, who was hearing negative reactions to her sudden shift in management style.

I've seen many managers with less gumption than Ms. Green give up under such circumstances. Many managers, after a rocky start like this one, think: "My boss isn't into this. My employees aren't into it. Maybe I'm not that good at it anyway. Maybe I can back out of this whole thing and go back to my familiar routine of hands-off management, until the next unnecessary crisis erupts."

But not Ms. Green. Ms. Green said: "OK. Let's try this again from the top." This time, there would be no lack of making the necessary preparations.

Seven Ways to Prepare Before You Reboot Your Management Style

1. **Prepare yourself psychologically**. Are you ready, willing, and able to commit the time, energy, effort, and consistency that it will take to change? Your role at work is going to change. Your relationships at work are going to change. Your experience at work is going

to change. You are going to be the person who is all about the work, who is setting people up for success every day, who is helping every person earn what she needs. Make sure you are sure. Expunge any of your own doubt first.

2. **Prepare yourself tactically.** The biggest impact of committing to highly engaged management is that you are putting a big chunk (or a couple of medium-sized chunks) of highly structured time into your daily schedule. That is what makes the whole thing work. If that big chunk of structured time is something that is not currently part of your day, you are going to have to get into the habit. Start building the habit in advance: find the one hour a day that works best for you, and set it aside every day for two weeks before you actually plunge into managing employees in one-on-one sessions. During those two weeks, use this one hour a day to continue with your preparations.

3. **Prepare yourself by gathering some intelligence on your employees.** What are all the things you really should have known all along? What are some things you'll need to keep in mind going forward? Gather information and start tuning in informally to your employees and their work. Stop shooting the breeze at work and start talking with your employees about the work. Start asking more questions. And do a lot of listening. You will get some surprises early on, no doubt. Some people will be put off that you are even asking. That's a good sign that you've been too hands-off until now. Some people will give vague answers. Others will tell you more than you would have guessed. You will start to learn who is doing what, where, why, when, and how.

4. **Start keeping a People List.** This is a running list (like the one I described near the end of Chapter One) of all the key people with whom you need to be engaged in a one-on-one dialogue right now. For each one of your direct reports, take note:

- When and where was your last conversation with that person? Regarding what?
- What should you be talking about with this person?

- When and where are you going to have your next conversation?
- What do you need to do to prepare in advance?

5. **Research possible tracking systems to monitor, measure, and document each employee's performance.** While your People List is a very good tool for remaining thoughtful and purposeful about your interactions with your direct reports, it is probably not a sufficient system for proper tracking of employee performance. Check with your HR to request tracking systems used by other teams or departments. You just need to be able to track, for each direct report, the expectations you are spelling out and how their concrete actions are lining up with those expectations, every step of the way. The most important thing about your tracking system is that you come up with a system that you will actually use—a system that works for you, that you can stick to. The sooner you figure that out, the better.

6. **Start working on a preliminary schedule for your regular one-on-ones.** When are you going to meet with each person and for how long? If you've been using one hour a day to prepare for this change in your management practices, then you are well on your way to making that hour-a-day management a habit. Now you need to decide how you are going to divide that time among your employees. (Remember that at first you may have to dedicate more time than one hour a day, perhaps even an hour and a half per day, until your one-on-one meetings become routine and brief.)

7. **Prepare your "Good news!" message.** You need to be prepared to discuss the impending management change with key people, including your boss. You don't want to act as if you've been failing as a manager until now. Instead, adopt a simple message: "Good news! I'm very committed to becoming a better manager, stronger and more highly engaged. Here's what that's going to look like. I'm going to build a regular, ongoing, structured one-on-one

dialogue with every person who reports to me." Remember, you are delivering good news! You are about to be spending a lot more time setting people up for success and helping them avoid unnecessary problems. You are going to provide more guidance and direction and support, helping your employees do better, work smarter and faster, and earn more rewards. That is good news! Make sure you feel that so it guides your tone every step of the way.

Once you've thoroughly prepared, it's time to go public!

The first person you should talk with is your own boss. Most bosses will be delighted to hear that you want to work hard to become a better manager and will be happy to help you in your efforts. If your boss is going to be an obstacle, it's better to find out immediately. Spell out for your boss exactly what you are trying to accomplish. Ask your boss if she supports your efforts. Explain that you will need her help and guidance.

The second time around, Ms. Green made sure at the outset to talk everything through in detail with her own boss. They realized that there were certain responsibilities on which they did not have exactly the same understanding of the standards and requirements. They didn't want to have different standards and requirements, so they went through them all to make sure they were on the same page, so that employees wouldn't be torn or confused.

Ms. Green told me, "My boss had been going around me and interacting directly with my employees. And even more the other way, my employees were going around me to my boss when they didn't like what I had to say. So we had to resolve that at the outset." Ms. Green and her boss decided together on ground rules for when and where and how each of them would meet with the employees. They agreed on what they would each discuss with those employees. And they agreed to make sure and talk regularly to ensure they were both conveying the same messages to Ms. Green's direct reports. They also decided that when Ms. Green's direct reports went directly to her boss, he would walk the employee back to Ms. Green's office so the three of them could discuss the matter together. The boss agreed in those cases to let Ms. Green handle the matter and to chime in only when necessary.

You don't need permission from your boss to be strong and highly engaged. But you definitely need your boss's support to be optimally successful. And it will be ideal if you have your boss's help when it comes to holding employees accountable, imposing negative consequences on low performers, and helping high performers earn special rewards. Do everything you can to keep your boss in the loop and highly supportive every step of the way in your journey to become a better and stronger manager.

Once you get your boss on board, you should consider other key partners and colleagues you need to apprise of any coming changes. Think about how the changes are going to affect the people with whom you interact routinely and who interact routinely with your employees. Whomever you need to prepare or enlist, sit down and talk with them, one by one. Tell them your plan. Ask for their support.

After all that preparation and all those advance discussions, it is time to announce to your team, "I'm going to be a better manager, and here's what that is going to look like." Get everybody together, and in the full light of public disclosure make a commitment to yourself and your team: "Good news! I am going to be a better manager. Here's what that means."

Be prepared for your employees to be concerned, to ask lots of questions, to second-guess you, and to doubt that you will follow through. It will take them a while to get used to it. A good way to end the team meeting is to schedule your initial one-on-one meeting with each person on the team.

Then, fully prepared, start doing your regular one-on-ones, one person at a time, one day at a time. In these, explain that this is a learning process for you and that you will make mistakes. Explain that you plan to revise and adjust your approach as you go forward. Let each person know that you understand this is a big change for her, too, and that you expect her to go through a learning process. Explain that you need her help in making this change work for both of you. Explain that you know you will get better and better at this new approach to your working relationship, and so will she.

After you've talked about why you are making this big change, the most important thing to discuss is the parameters of the regular one-on-one dialogue you will have with each person from now on:

How often will you meet with this person?
Exactly when and for how long?
Where?

Make sure the person understands that you are 100 percent committed to this new approach, but that you are also flexible. The best way to end this initial meeting is to reiterate your plans for the next meeting: When? Where? How long? What will you talk about? Your schedule will take shape gradually as you start managing closely. Thereafter, you will probably negotiate times with each person on an ongoing basis. Over time, you and the people you manage will get better and better at using the meetings to get what you need from each other.

EPILOGUE

Now that you've read this book, I hope you are inspired (or at least motivated) to dedicate (or rededicate) yourself to practicing the fundamentals of management with rigor and consistency.

If you read the book from beginning to end, you have seen case after case in which it's clear that things go wrong because the manager is managing on autopilot, engaging mostly in relatively unstructured, low-substance, and hit-or-miss communication. Having read this book, you should never again allow yourself to be one of those managers.

Through reading about one challenge after another, I hope you've fully appreciated how the most effective managers apply the fundamentals of management to gain control of any situation and how the solution unfolds in the process. The solution to nearly every problem comes from consistently practicing the fundamentals, very well. That means maintaining an ongoing schedule of high-quality, one-on-one dialogues with every single person you manage.

If you consistently practice the fundamentals, I guarantee that you will quickly see results: increased employee performance and morale, increased retention of high performers, increased turnover among low performers, and significant, measurable improvements in business outcomes. Not only that, but you will find yourself spending a steadily diminishing amount of your management time on "firefighting."

I know it is not easy to practice the fundamentals with rigor and consistency. To get going, you need to overcome three big hurdles:

First, you have to make the transition, which may require that you find new reserves of energy, conviction, and follow-through. Going from *not* maintaining high-structure, high-substance, ongoing, one-on-one dialogues with every direct report to establishing that practice requires you to change personally and professionally, communicate this to colleagues and superiors, roll it out to direct reports, and then start doing it.

Second, you'll find it's time-consuming, especially at first. Getting back to fundamentals usually requires a big up-front investment of extra time. If you haven't been doing it before, you will still have to fight all the fires you have not prevented at the same time you are heavily investing time in preventing future fires. This could take up twice as much of your time for a while, until all the old fires die out.

Third, you need to stay ahead of the vicious cycle. You have to use discipline and focus to consistently spend your management time where it should be spent—up front, every step of the way, *before* anything goes right, wrong, or average.

If you commit to this—consistently maintaining the high-structure, high-substance, ongoing, one-on-one dialogues—in a matter of weeks everything will get much better. Plus, you will start getting your time back.

Of course, the really hard part is truly sticking close to the fundamentals even when the heat is on. Don't let that crisis throw you off your game. And when you do run across a difficult challenge, just remember, it is probably dealt with in this book. So please keep it on your desk. It is intentionally designed to be used and reused as situations arise—a hands-on management tool you can return to over and over throughout your career as a leader, manager, supervisor.

And if you find yourself slipping away from the fundamentals—if you have a bad day, week, month, or year—just bounce back. Get back on your game and start practicing the fundamentals again, with rigor and consistency, one person at time, one day at a time.

The fundamentals are all you need.

ACKNOWLEDGMENTS

This book is the outcome of what is now twenty years of workplace research. At this point, hundreds of thousands of individuals have contributed to our surveys, interviews, and focus groups since we first began our workplace research in 1993. First and foremost, I want to thank every single one of you from the bottom of my heart for sharing the wisdom of your experience with us! Without you there would be no RainmakerThinking, Inc., and this book surely would not exist.

Thanks also to the very many business leaders who bring me in to learn from and help your managers facing the real challenges every day in the real world. To the hundreds of thousands who have attended my keynote addresses and seminars: thanks for listening, for laughing, for sharing the wisdom of your experience, for pushing me with the really tough questions, for your kindness, and for teaching me. My greatest intellectual debt is to the managers who have participated in our boot camps—I've learned so much from helping them wrestle with their very real management problems in the real world. Special thanks to those managers whose real stories appear in this book; I've mixed up the ancillary details to help keep the stories anonymous.

To my now retired partners in RainmakerThinking—Jeff Coombs and Carolyn Martin—thank you for your hard work and commitment and your valuable contributions to this enterprise. I love you both and consider you both close and true friends. I am deeply grateful for the life-altering experience of working with each one of you.

To our very dear old friends and my new business partners, Chris Glowacki and Kristin Campbell, and their entire family to the furthest extent of consanguinity, but especially their children, Lily, Albert, Herbie, and Stella: this book is dedicated to you all.

Chris is a long-time media executive and a seasoned entrepreneur. I know that his ability, skill, knowledge, wisdom, and energy are going to take us to the next level. Chris and his team will allow us to broaden and deepen our research; to deliver our message to a much larger audience; and bring our best practices, tools, and techniques to many more leaders and managers. He is also an extraordinary individual.

Krissy is a formidable entrepreneur in her own right, having invented and developed the first electronic higher education applications system in the early 1990s. And you should see her Christmas cookie operation—it rivals any commercial bakery I've ever seen. Krissy brings to our mission her keen intelligence and insight, meticulous organization, clear candid communication, spectacular charisma, and good cheer—and she gets things done!

To Chris and Krissy and their children, all of whom consented to being uprooted and transplanted about a half mile from the RainmakerThinking headquarters in New Haven: Thank you! I am deeply grateful. Your family is our family. We love you all, every one.

To Susan Ingraham, my longtime executive assistant (and one of the most reliable, considerate, even-tempered, and good-hearted people I have ever known): thank you so much for everything you do, Susan. I honestly don't know what I would do without you. You have my undying gratitude and loyalty.

Now, to the publisher and the editors:

To everyone at Wiley and Jossey-Bass: Thanks to every one of you who has put your faith and good thinking and hard work into the books we have done together, especially this one. Special thanks to Susan Williams, formerly executive editor at Jossey-Bass.

Genoveva Llosa, my brilliant former editor for three books in a row, has moved on to a new publishing house, but not before helping me fashion the initial proposal for this book. I am immensely grateful to Genoveva for all she has taught me over the years.

My brilliant current editor, Karen Murphy, has made this book so very much better. She adopted me and this project with kindness and conviction and steered me to one excellent choice after another. Then she took the way-too-long manuscript I sent her and transformed it into a leaner and stronger book without losing any of the content whatsoever. Readers can also thank her for the more user-friendly chapter organization and the easier-to-digest sentences. On behalf of our readers, Karen, thank you so very much for all of your excellent work.

Great thanks also to Kristi Hein, copyeditor, who did stellar work fixing the language, grammar, logic, and continuity of the copy and added some great ideas. Readers will enjoy the book much more thanks to Kristi!

Then I always come to Susan Rabiner, who not only is a world-class literary agent for me and also for my wife, Debby, but also has become one of our very most favorite people in the world. It is not an overstatement to say that Susan Rabiner understands nonfiction book publishing as well as or better than anybody else in the world. She is simply the smartest and the best. She and her husband, the late genius Al Fortunato, wrote the book about writing and publishing nonfiction, *Thinking Like Your Editor: How to Write Great Serious Nonfiction—and Get It Published*. Susan is 100 percent responsible for my success as a writer. How can I thank Susan enough?

My family and friends are the anchors of meaning in my life. First, thanks to my parents, Norma Propp Tulgan and Henry Tulgan, for raising me as well as you did. I love you both very much; you are among my very closest friends to this day, and I treasure the time we spend together.

Thanks to my parents-in-law, Julie and Paul Applegate; my nieces and nephews (from oldest to youngest): Elisa, Joseph, Perry, Erin, Frances, and Eli; my sister, Ronna, and my brother, Jim; my sister-in-law, Tanya, and my brothers-in-law, Shan and Tom. I love every one of you very, very much.

I always add a special extra thanks to my niece Frances because, due to the fortuities of life, I have always thought of her as if she were my own child.

Finally, I always reserve my last and most profound thanks for my wife, Debby Applegate. Among her many impressive credentials, Debby won the 2007 Pulitzer Prize for her biography of Henry Ward Beecher! Can you believe that? In short, Debby is a world-class talent among world-class talents. And she's all mine! We fell in love in September 1985 and we've been together ever since. Anybody who knows me knows darned well that I'm not exaggerating when I say that I have always been and always will be completely awestruck by Debby. Anybody who doesn't know Debby, well . . . you just have to meet her to even begin to understand. There is nothing—absolutely nothing—I have done since the day I met Debby that has not been profoundly influenced by her. Debby is my constant adviser, my toughest critic, my closest collaborator, the love of my life, my best friend, my smartest friend, my partner in all things, half of my soul, owner of my heart, and the person without whom I would cease to be.

Bruce Tulgan is an adviser to business leaders all over the world and a sought-after keynote speaker and seminar leader. He is the founder and CEO of RainmakerThinking, Inc., a management research and training firm, as well as RainmakerThinking.Training, an online training company. Bruce is the author of numerous books, including the best-selling *It's Okay to Be the Boss* (2007), the classic *Managing Generation X* (1995), *Not Everyone Gets a Trophy* (2009), *It's Okay to Manage Your Boss* (2010), and *FAST Feedback* (1999). His work has been the subject of thousands of news stories around the world. He has written pieces for numerous publications, including the *New York Times*, *USA Today*, the *Harvard Business Review*, *Training* magazine, and *Human Resources*. Bruce also holds a fifth-degree black belt in classical Okinawan Uechi Ryu karate. He lives in New Haven, Connecticut, with his wife, Dr. Debby Applegate, author of the Pulitzer Prize–winning biography *The Most Famous Man in America: The Biography of Henry Ward Beecher* (2006), as well as *Madam: The Notorious Life and Times of Polly Adler* (2015). Bruce can be reached by email at brucet@rainmakerthinking.com.

INDEX